CONTENTS

KU-498-403

YAR

MAHATMA GANDHI

A BEGINNER'S GUIDE

GENEVIEVE BLAIS, M.S.W.

Hodder & Stoughton

A MEMBER OF THE HODDER HEADLINE GROUP

Dedication

This book is dedicated to my Spiritual Teacher and True Heart-Master Avatar Adi Da Samraj

Orders: please contact Bookpoint Ltd, 39 Milton Park, Abingdon, Oxon OX14 4TD. Telephone: (44) 01235 827720, Fax: (44) 01235 400454. Lines are open from 9.00–6.00, Monday to Saturday, with a 24-hour message answering service. Email address: orders@bookpoint.co.uk

British Library Cataloguing in Publication Data
A catalogue record for this title is available from The British Library

ISBN 0 340 790350

First published 2000
Impression number   10 9 8 7 6 5 4 3 2 1
Year   2005 2004 2003 2002 2001

Copyright © 2000 Genevieve Blais
Series editors Rob Abbott and Charlie Bell

Illustrations by Steve Coots
Typeset by Transet Limited, Coventry, England.
Printed in Great Britain for Hodder & Stoughton Educational, a division of Hodder Headline Plc, 338 Euston Road, London NW1 3BH by Cox & Wyman, Reading, Berks

Contents

Introduction

Mahatma Gandhi was born Mohandas Karamchand Gandhi on 2 October, 1869 in the northwestern Indian seaport town of Porbandar. He was not born into greatness, but he certainly achieved it within his lifetime. His renown did not come from personal ambition, but from his heart-felt desire to help all who were discriminated against, and to take a stand against intolerance everywhere.

The name Mahatma, which means 'Great Soul', was given to him because of his extraordinary quest for morality, justice and spirituality. He saw himself as a man who could not follow rules that oppressed human rights and felt it his duty to help make new ones. To some, he was considered one of the greatest political figures and negotiators of his era. To others, he was considered a saint. He said of himself, however, that he was neither. He considered himself to be an ordinary seeker of the truth and a religious man, but not a guru or holy man.

He advocated social change and tolerance. His belief was that everyone should be afforded the same rights and privileges in order to shape their own lives. He was vehemently opposed to all forms of oppression and bigotry, whether social, religious or cultural. He devoted his career to the removal of discrimination and injustice. Gandhi also advocated *ahimsa*, or non-killing. In whatever he undertook, he did it with passive resistance. In situations that would test even the strongest of wills, he was able to remain constant in this practice of non-violence. He would rather experience hardship than resort to force as a means of resolution. He was willing to put his own life at stake for the good of all and he became well-known for his use of fasting as a form of political protest.

He did not preach what he did not himself practise. He undertook many experiments with diet, politics, and community living and started a movement called the *satyagraha*, a term he invented meaning 'firmness in truth'. In private and in public he tested his morality as a character, his determination and his beliefs. Though his lifestyle was austere, he was a very cheerful man, full of love and compassion. He believed that there was no point in creating political and social change if people's hearts were not also transformed.

Gandhi was an enigma in his own time. He was neither a priest nor a prime minister, yet his imaginative thinking and charisma gained him worldwide recognition and millions of followers. He was a man of great intent and modesty. One of his greatest achievements was the large part he played in the gaining of independence for India in 1947 from British rule. He did not do this out of rancour for the British and, in fact, considered himself a loyal subject of Britain for most of his life. He pursued the idea of home rule so that India could take control of her own destiny. When India was split into two countries because of the irrevocable difficulties between Muslims and Hindus, he felt there was little to celebrate. His purpose, and ultimate goal was a peaceful co-existence. It was not the happy ending that he had hoped for.

To fully understand Mahatma Gandhi and his non-violent fight for justice. *An Autobiography, Or, The Story of My Experiments with Truth* (see Further Reading).

Mahatma Gandhi's Early Years and Education

*My life has been an open book. I have no
secrets and I encourage no secrets.*

M.K. Gandhi

Mahatma Gandhi (born Mohandas Karamchand Gandhi on 2
October, 1869) became one of his country's most prominent figures in
the twentieth century and was later deemed the 'Father of a Nation' by
his supporters. His life story is one of a modest man whose drive for
social reform transformed him into one of the world's most notable
champions of human rights.

Gandhi as a young boy.

THE GANDHI FAMILY

In **Hindu** tradition, one is born into a
particular social class (caste) and it is highly
irregular, if not impossible, to move between
castes. The Gandhi family belonged to the
Modh Banias, or middle caste. People of this
caste are generally thought to be merchants. This makes it unusual that

the Gandhi family had for generations assumed roles as 'prime ministers' in their local region. Even though they were not of a high caste, they were respected leaders in their community. Karamchand Gandhi, Mohandas's father, was a member of a local court that handled disputes between chiefs and their clansmen. He had had no formal education but was a fair man and was highly regarded throughout the village. Mohandas's description of his father was that of a man who was 'truthful, brave and generous'. As was the case with Mohandas, his father held no desire for wealth or prestige and acquired few material possessions.

Gandhi's father, having been widowed three times, was into his fourth marriage when Mohandas was born. Mohandas was the youngest child of Karamchand and Putlibai Gandhi. He was a shy, sensitive child who was devoted to his parents. Throughout his life he had a great deal of respect for his elders and their morality. This, along with his uncompromising integrity, would be among his trademark qualities.

Although Gandhi was born to a Hindu family, his father had very little religious training. His mother was, however, very constant in her religious practices. Her piety and dedication to the Hindu religion made a lasting impression

KEYWORD

Atheism rejection of belief in God or gods.

on Mohandas, and his spiritual quest was generated from her faith. However, as he developed his own spiritual identity he did not consider himself a Hindu. He even spent some of his youth pondering **atheism**. He regarded himself to be a man seeking God, but not being attached to any particular religion, although many of his customs stemmed from Hindu practices and beliefs.

CHILDHOOD MARRIAGE

As Mohandas's father got older, he wanted to make sure that Mohandas's future was established, and so he arranged a marriage for him. This was done without Mohandas's knowledge or consent. Child marriages were part of the Hindu tradition in Indian society during this period. So at the age of 14 Mohandas married Kasturbai, the daughter of his father's good friend, who was only 13 years of age.

Mohandas was not particularly mature at 14 and was certainly ill-equipped to take on the role of a husband.

As we will see later, he had a lot of regret for how he treated his wife in the early years of their marriage. Even though he was formally married, the custom of the time was for the bride to continue to live a good portion of her time at the home of her parents. Gandhi remarked later in life that this situation helped his relationship with his wife a great deal because he was too immature to create a mature relationship at such a young age. Later in his career, he would make the abolishment of child marriages one of his top priorities.

TEENAGE REBELLION

As with most teenagers, Mohandas rebelled against his elders by experimenting with what was forbidden to him. He was trying to find himself in a world in which he had had to grow up very quickly. One of the things that always set Mohandas and his family apart, was that they did not let their Hindu roots keep them from having friendships with people of all castes and religions. He was taught a sincere tolerance and love for people of different religions and backgrounds.

Mohandas spent a great deal of his rebellious years with his good friend Sheikh Mehtab who was a **Muslim**. Together they experimented with eating meat, smoking and drinking alcohol, all of which are forbidden in both the Hindu and Muslim faiths.

KEYWORD

Muslim a follower of the religion of Islam, second-most prominent religion in India.

Gandhi's family did not like Sheikh or the influence he had on Mohandas. To rationalize their escapades together, Mohandas deluded himself into thinking that he was going to convert Sheikh to a more 'moral' lifestyle, but he hadn't sufficiently resolved his own opinions on these forbidden pleasures yet and continued his experimentation in secret for a few more years. As with any exploration, Mohandas eventually came to his own conclusions about his choices based on what felt right for him. He decided to refrain from the use of all of them.

GANDHI AS A STUDENT

Mohandas was not a brilliant student, but his teachers liked him. His bashfulness made the classroom an uneasy place for him and as soon as his lessons were over he would run home as quickly as possible. He did his lessons more out of respect for his teachers than out of interest in his work. Mohandas was surprised at some of the merit certificates he gained, as he did not think himself a particularly good student. He did not mind whether he was considered intelligent and often underestimated his aptitude. What was more important to him was that people regarded him as a decent and honorable character.

He didn't like sports and had a difficult time with them being a mandatory part of his education. He was too timid to enjoy the competitiveness of the lessons and would get out of them as often as possible. But he did love taking long walks, and later in his life he would become an advocate of regular exercise.

His early marriage set him back a year at school, and he had to catch up. This was arduous for Mohandas, and he even thought of leaving school altogether at one stage, but his teachers encouraged him, so he continued. Again, he did so more out of reverence for them than out of a desire to complete his education. He couldn't bear the thought of letting down those he respected.

THE DEATH OF HIS FATHER

Gandhi has expressed a great deal of grief and shame over the death of his father. This is, in part, because of his love for his father, but also because of where he was at the time of his death.

When his father became gravely ill, when Mohandas was 16, he nursed him. One afternoon, while giving his father a massage, Gandhi was thinking about Kasturbai, his wife. When he finished the massage, he went home to sleep with his wife. While he was in bed with her, he received word that his father had died and he felt repentant that he had not been with his father in his last moments. The shame of this stayed with him all his life. He also felt bad because at the time his wife was pregnant, and not long after this she gave birth to a son who only lived a few days. Mohandas felt that his behaviour in both instances was much less than honorable. He has referred to these events as his 'double shame'.

A DECISION TO GO TO ENGLAND

After passing his examinations in 1887, Mohandas was expected to attend college. Because his family were not wealthy, it was decided that he should go to the nearest college to home. He joined his new school, but soon found himself at a loss with the work. He felt that he could not relate to the courses he was taking and was not able to concentrate on them. Disheartened and uninterested, he returned home.

He was advised by a good friend of the family that he still needed to continue his education. Everyone felt it was crucial that he train to take up a post of responsibility. Times had changed and it would not be possible to take up any dignified post, such as a Diwan (town official) as his father had done, unless he was educated. His family thought that a law degree would be a good choice. However, procuring a law degree in India would take Mohandas four or five years, and he felt this was too long. He could receive a degree in three years if he were to go to England. He decided to go.

This decision created a lot of upheaval within his family and caste. For one thing, sponsorship would be hard to find for such an expensive undertaking. Mohandas's older brother thought it was a worthwhile investment and felt it would be a post that would bring respect to their family. His mother though, and other members of their caste, thought it was an appalling idea. They felt Mohandas would not be able to practise Hinduism in England because he would be so far away from his culture and religious affiliations. They also felt he would be lured into a life of eating meat and drinking alcohol.

Mohandas took more advice from his uncle and another family advisor. He knew if his uncle gave his blessing that his mother would also. He did not want to go without his mother's agreement. In order to get his mother's approval, he vowed to avoid wine, women and meat.

As with many things in Gandhi's life, his decision to go to England was a double-edged sword. While he was given a supportive send-off, his caste made it clear, that if he decided to go, he would be excommunicated. Gandhi chose to stand by his decision to go.

COMING OF AGE IN A FOREIGN LAND

Mohandas Gandhi considered himself a loyal part of the **British Empire** and wanted to learn as much about it as possible. In London he readily assumed new social manners and customs: he began eating with a knife and forks; he took lessons in elocution, dancing and the violin; he experimented with comportment and dressed himself in only the most fashionable clothing.

KEYWORDS

British Empire, the United Kingdom and the territories under its control.

Socialism, economic theory or system in which the means of production, distribution and exchange are owned by the community collectively.

His time in England was instrumental in his development. It began a learning process for him that matured his character and belief system. One concern he had was how he was going to with fit into Western culture without losing his Indian heritage. He had already jumped impetuously into new styles and ways of behaving, and there were, of course, the temptations of meat, alcohol and women all around him.

It was an exciting and testing time for him, but he was determined not to break his vows of abstinence. One of his saving graces was coming upon the Vegetarian Society, with which he became ardently involved. His commitment to vegetarianism had now become one of personal choice rather than what was expected of him.

He immersed himself in many types of debate over East–West relations. He became interested in a number of movements from the industrial revolution and women's liberation, to pro-ecology and **socialism**. He studied theories of civil disobedience and was impressed by the writings of **Thoreau, Tolstoy**, and **Marx**. All of this learning aided in shaping the crusader he was to become. It also helped to bring him back to his roots so that he did not assimilate himself completely into British culture.

Mohandas also became interested in the **Theosophical Society**. This was founded in the United States in 1875 by **Madame Blavatsky**, among others, to promote a system of philosophic and religious thought which included mystic insight. Theosophy is based on the concept that true knowledge comes not only from reason but from direct communion with divine reality. It incorporates the Hindu and Buddhist concepts of karma and rein- carnation into its teaching.

KEYWORDS

Thoreau (Henry David) (1817–62), American author who wrote about civil disobedience.

Tolstoy (Leo) (1829–1910), Russian author and playwright.

Marx (Karl) (1818–83), developed the concept of socialism.

Theosophical Society, modern religious move- ment based on intuition and spiritual ecstacy

Madame Blavatsky, one of the founders of the Theosophical Society.

While participating in the Theosophical Society in London, Gandhi met Annie Besant who was a prominent leader of the movement. She was also a social reformer and interested in Indian culture. She went on to found the India Home Rule League in 1916, and devoted much of her life to the Indian struggle for independence. When asked if he would like to join the Theosophical Society, Gandhi declined saying that he had very little knowledge of his own religion and did not want to become attached to any religious body.

Still only twenty years old, he began investigating many different options in dietetics, hygiene and economy. Everything was a new experiment for him. He scrupulously looked at all his options from a medical, practical, scientific and ethical point of view.

RETURNING TO INDIA

By 1891 Gandhi had earned his law degree, but still felt he was not ready to practise law. He was however, happy to be going home, and was especially looking forward to seeing his mother again. On his return home he learned that his beloved mother had passed away. His brother had kept the news from him, thinking it would be too difficult for Mohandas to hear this on his own so far away from his family.

The next two years were not easy. He had lost both his parents, his wife had matured, and he also had two sons to look after. After such high hopes of a bright future, he was also having trouble finding employment. So when he met a South African businessman who offered him work, he took it. In 1893 he left his growing family and journeyed to South Africa, which was also a part of the British Empire at that time.

✳ ✳ ✳ ✳ SUMMARY ✳ ✳ ✳ ✳

- Mahatma Gandhi was born Mohandas Karamchand Gandhi on 2 October 1869.

- His family belonged to the middle Hindu caste called the Modh Banias.

- His father, Karamchand Gandhi, was a 'prime minister' for his locality.

- He was married at the age of 14 to Kasturbai, who was 13.

- He was very upset by the death of his father and felt guilty that he was not with him at the time he died.

- He left for England at the age of 18 to study in law.

- In England he became a member of the Vegetarian Society and began reading discourses on civil disobedience and social reform.

- On his return to India in 1891 he discovered that his beloved mother had died.

- In 1893, after having difficulty finding work, he left his family for a job in South Africa.

India – Its History and Culture

A nation's culture resides in the hearts and in the soul of its people.

M.K. Gandhi

India is a country of many contrasts, geographically, economically, culturally and socially. Its 880 million habitants make it the second most densely populated country in the world, with 16 per cent of the world's population. It is the largest **democracy** in the world. The official languages are English and Hindi.

Cut off by the Himalayan mountains to the north, it forms its own **subcontinent**. The weather and terrain vary considerably over its vast 1,270,350 square miles. The climate in the north tends to be cooler and drier and sees more seasonal changes. The south has a more static, hot and humid climate, which gives way to incredible rainfall during monsoon.

KEYWORDS

Democracy, a country governed by its people through their elected representatives.

Subcontinent, a large land mass that is a distinct part of a continent.

ANCIENT HISTORY

India's roots date back to 3,000 BCE. It has weathered numerous invasions and migrations throughout its development, and it is the influence of diverse civilizations converging over the centuries that has helped to create the complex and rich culture we now consider to be uniquely Indian.

The first known people to have lived in India are the Indus Valley civilization dating from 2,500 BCE. Scientists have discovered that they had a system of writing, counting, measuring and weighing. They are thought to have been a grain-growing culture which was destroyed because of environmental changes such as floods.

The next significant cultural influence was brought about by the migration of the Aryans from Central Asia in 1500 BCE. When the Aryans arrived in India they found a tribe of people called the Dravidians who lived in towns and farmed the land. The Aryans tended to be more **nomadic**, tending sheep, goats, cows and horses. They established themselves as rulers and drove many of the Dravidians to the south. The Aryans brought with them the ancient language of Sanskrit and the religious rituals and texts of the Vedas. During their period of reign, the most important of Hindu scriptures, the Upanishads, also appeared. They also introduced the idea of the caste system which would become more refined in time.

KEYWORD

Nomadic, wandering from place to place (to find pasture and food).

In 326 BCE, Alexander the Great arrived in what is now Pakistan. He did not advance any further, however, because his troops were worn out and suffering disease.

Following in Alexander's footsteps was Chandra-gupta Maurya who established the Mauryan Empire, which extended over most of northern India, parts of Asia and what is now Afghanistan. His grandson, Ashoka, became one of India's most famous emperors. He ruled from 272–232 BCE. Initially he was a warring commander who took over the country by force, but when he saw the death and destruction that he had caused, he was stricken with remorse. From that point, he governed with a philosophy of non-violence and converted to **Buddhism**, helping to spread its message throughout the land.

KEYWORD

Buddhism, a religious belief whereby man seeks enlightenment by denying greed, hatred and delusion and other causes of suffering.

The ensuing period in India's history was governed by the Gupta dynasty between 320–500 CE. This period is often referred to as India's Golden Age because of the prodigious development of art, literature, mathematics, philosophy and science that occurred. It was during this dynasty that many of the Hindu temples were built and the system of medicine called Ayurveda was developed.

The next substantial culture to emerge was the Mogul empire. It was led by Babur in 1526. He was a Muslim leader who came from central Asia. His grandson, Akbar, became the greatest of all the Mogul rulers. Although he was a Muslim, he governed with great tolerance and made many Hindus officials within the government and military.

Akbar's grandson, Shah Jahan, ruled from 1628–58 and built a new capital city in Delhi. He was responsible for many great pieces of architecture, including the Taj Mahal, which is considered to be one of the seven wonders of the world. His son, Aurangzeb, contributed to the demise of the Mogul empire by forcibly trying to convert Hindus to Islam, destroying Hindu temples and levying high taxes. This gave Europeans an opening to begin to take control of certain areas of India.

The Taj Mahal built by the Mogul Emperor Shah Jahan and considered to be one of the Seven Wonders of the World.

The final ruling elite were the British, and this will be looked at in greater detail in the following chapter.

RELIGIOUS INFLUENCE

India is a very religious country and its culture and customs are derived from religious beliefs. Unfortunately, much of its history is coloured with religious intolerance.

India comprises 83 per cent Hindus, 11 per cent Muslims, 2 per cent **Sikhs**, 2 per cent Christians and 2 per cent other denominations including Buddhists, **Jains**, **Parsees**, and **Jews**.

The two main religions of India are briefly outlined below.

Hinduism

Hinduism is the most prominent religion of India. Its history is long and complex and has evolved over the centuries, assimilating its theology from both the Indus civilization and the Aryan culture.

Hindus call God by the name Brahman. They believe that Brahman is the supreme spirit or being, but they have many other deities which they worship. Many of these are derived from nature.

The **dharma** is taken from the body of literature called the Vedas. The knowledge found in the Vedas was considered to be directly inspired from a non-human source. Originally the concepts and stories were transferred from the **sages** down the years by word of mouth. When it became a written scripture it was in Sanskrit. The Vedas are key to understanding the concepts of Hinduism.

A very basic explanation of Vedic dharma is:

* Everything in existence is an expression of God.

* Everyone's life goal is to come closer to God.

* Worldly desires keep a person distracted and hence keep them away from knowing God (we will see how this idea in particular is one that Mahatma Gandhi followed).

KEYWORDS

Sikh, a follower of Sikkism created by a Hindu named Nanak in 1469 who criticized Hindu and Muslim teaching.

Jain, a person whose religion is Jainism, an ancient religion founded in India.

Parsee, a person whose religion is Zoroastrianism, which was founded by an ancient Persian prophet named Zoroaster.

Jew, a person whose religion is Judaism; a member of the Semitic people descended from the ancient Israelites.

Dharma, a custom regarded as a religious and moral duty.

Sage, someone revered for their profound wisdom.

In Hinduism it is believed that everyone has a soul and that the soul never dies. They believe in the law of **karma**, so that a good deed will be rewarded, and causing harm will be punished. Hindus also believe in **reincarnation**.

Hindus are born into a caste system and cannot move from that caste system during the course of their current lifetime. The caste system provides an outline for what will become their social, cultural and religious expectations and associations. Numerous times over the years, attempts have been made to abolish or change the caste system, but it still remains an integral part of Hindu culture.

There are four main paths a person can take in order to get closer to Brahman. The first is through prayer and devotion to a deity. The second is to do good or behave, in all aspects of life, for the betterment of society. The third is the path of knowledge. This is an intellectual path to God and requires having a teacher or guide. The fourth path is the path of **yoga**. This path is for disciplining the body and the mind. All of these paths are considered to be equal to each other and they are not separate. One would generally combine one or more of the paths in the quest for spiritual development.

Hindus believe there are four fundamental stages to life. The first is the **celibate** student, the second is the householder (getting married, raising children etc), the third is becoming a **hermit**, or forest dweller, and the fourth is becoming a sannyasin, or wandering **ascetic**. It is assumed that not many people will aspire or be able to move into the third or fourth stages of life.

KEYWORDS

Ascetic, a person who practises self-denial (especially for religious purposes).

Celibate, a person who abstains from sex.

Hermit, a person living in solitude.

Karma, a principle of retributive justice for past deeds.

Reincarnation, rebirth.

Yoga, the Hindu system of philosophy aimed at uniting the self with the Supreme Being through physical and mental exercises.

Islam

Islam is the second-most prominent religion that has influenced India's society. It is a **Semitic** religion that has its roots in Judaism and Christianity. People who follow the

KEYWORD

Semitic, of Arabic and Judaic origins.

religion of Islam are called Muslims, which literally translated means 'one who submits to God'. They call God by the name Allah.

Islam was founded by the prophet Muhammad. He was not considered to be the incarnation of the Divine, but the messenger of God. For Muslims, he is the greatest of all prophets who have ever lived. He was born in 570 BCE in Mecca. When he was forty years old, he had his first spiritual revelations, and it was from them that he created the Koran, the holy book of Islam. It is written as poetry and came to Muhammad in visions where the angel Gabriel appeared to him. Muhammad died in 632 BCE not long after he had declared that he had finished what he felt he was put on earth to accomplish.

The Koran provides not only a guide to spiritual practice, but also defines appropriate social and political views and behaviour.

Muslims believe that doing good in this life will bring rewards in heaven.

There are five pillars of Islam on which religious practice is based:

* Professing one's faith and true intention.
* Actively worshipping – praying up to five times a day.
* Giving of alms – this can mean giving of one's time and energies as well as giving money.
* Fasting – each year Muslims undertake a fast of thirty days during a period called Ramadan. They are not allowed to eat anything between sunrise and sunset during this time, nor are they allowed to smoke, drink water or have sex.
* Going on a pilgrimage – the most important pillar of Islam is a pilgrimage to Mecca. Most Muslims try to do this at least once in their lives.

Muslims also abstain from eating pork, drinking wine, gambling or lending money.

MODERN INDIA

India has always been awash with many contrasts. As it has moved into the modern world, many of these have become much more pronounced. Thirty per cent of its population live in rural areas. The same percentage live below the bread line. In Bombay alone, over 100,000 people live destitute on the streets. At the other end of the spectrum, the middle classes have servants to wait on them.

The extremes of wealth are not the only discrepancies. A largely agricultural nation, it has its own nuclear weapons programme and suffers many problems with deforestation due to modernization.

India has only been a democracy since 1947 and two of its first prime ministers were assassinated. The hostility between Muslim and Hindu communities continues to be a source of violence and political unrest.

✳ ✳ ✳SUMMARY ✳ ✳ ✳

- India is a country of many contrasts, geographically, socially, economically and culturally.

- India is the second most populated country in the world with 880 million people.

- It has weathered numerous invasions and migrations throughout its development.

- The original inhabitants were called the Indus Valley civilization.

- In India, 83 per cent of the population are Hindus and 11 per cent are Muslims.

- India has only been a democracy since 1947.

- Conflicts between Muslims and Hindus remain one of India's biggest political and social problems.

3 Britain's Role in the History of India

We may have our private opinions but why should they be a bar to the meeting of hearts?

M.K. Gandhi

The Moguls were the last great Eastern ruling class of India. The founder of the Mogul dynasty was Babar, whose empire reigned from approximately 1526–1858. As was mentioned in chapter 2, India's history has incorporated migrations of other peoples, most of whom wanted to expand their kingdoms and take advantage of India's natural resources and wealth. The Europeans were no different in this respect. India was seen as an exotic land with many specialties to offer the West, including, spices, tea, silk and cotton, which they could export to their own countries.

Initially, only the very richest could afford these exotic items, but as trade grew and Europeans put down roots in India, many things from Indian culture gradually became part of Western life. Tea is a very good example of this – it has become a symbol for England although its source was originally India.

Europeans began to appear in India in the sixteenth century. The first to arrive was a Portuguese explorer named Vasco da Gama. At the time, Portugal was competing with the Italians for control over trade with Asian countries. The Portuguese gained control over some of the Western coast of India at this time, but did not extend themselves much further. The Dutch and French were next to travel to India, also looking for trade opportunities.

BRITISH EAST INDIA COMPANY

British interest in India was not far behind. Queen Elizabeth I (1533–1603) granted a charter in 1600 for a company to be formed called the East India Company. Its purpose was to establish trade links with India and supply England with exports. They had an agreement with the Mogul emperor, Jahangir, to set up trading posts in Bombay, Calcutta and Madras as a commercial venture. As time went on, England became the most prolific trading power in India and the East India Company began to gain a foothold in India that was to have political as well as a business implications.

France was the only other country to have firm trading roots in India. These were concentrated mainly in the south of India and so the French did not have the same power over Indian affairs that the English had acquired.

THE EIGHTEENTH CENTURY

Over the next 100 years, the influence of the British began to take hold. What began as a business venture turned into a bid for political control. By the mid-eighteenth century the power of the Mogul empire was ebbing away.

ROBERT CLIVE

In 1757, an agent for the East India Company named Robert Clive led an army in a battle at Plassey to defeat the Mogul governor of Bengal. Many historians consider this to be the turning point in the establishment of England as the ruling class in India. In 1774, Warren Hastings was appointed as the company's first Governor General of India. For the next 100 years, the British expanded their territorial control and political influence.

THE SEPOY MUTINY

The Indians were becoming resentful of the manoeuvring of the British, who had become a major interference in their lives. The British had imposed taxes on farmers, were confiscating land, and were generally making their presence felt. Indians felt that their culture and customs were at risk, and began to rebel. In 1857, a **mutiny** began at an army base near Delhi and quickly spread throughout the north and centre of India. It was called the Sepoy Mutiny.

KEYWORDS

Mutiny, a rebellion against authority.

Viceroy, the governor of a colony or province who rules in the name of the government.

It is said that the incident which began the rebellion was to do with the gun cartridges that the Indians were given to use in their guns, as defenders of the British Raj. In those days one had to bite open a cartridge before it could be used. The natives had heard that the cartridges were greased with cow and hog fat. This was an insult to both Hindus and Muslims. The cow is sacred to Hindus, and Muslims are not allowed to eat pork. It was one of the few times in India's history when Muslims and Hindus joined forces to fight the British.

The Indians were poor and inadequately armed or organized. It was not difficult for the British to squash their rebellion. By 1859, the Sepoy Mutiny showed the British that they could be facing a serious threat to their presence and that they needed to become efficiently consolidated if they wanted to remain in control.

THE BRITISH RAJ

In 1858, the British decided to govern India. This marked the beginning of what was to be known as the British Raj. Raj means administration or rule. Parliament became involved and took over all the holdings of the East India Company. It also took control of all the regional areas the company had been controlling.

A **viceroy** was appointed to be the official administrator in India. He then appointed an executive council to work with him. For each province in India, a British governor was appointed to act as head. Each governor in turn had their own executive council to help them legislate British control.

In 1876 Queen Victoria (1819–1901) was given the title Empress of India. She was never to set foot in there, but during her reign, the British began building roads and telegraph and telephone systems throughout the country. They also produced a vast network of railroads. In addition, the British had an interest in improving agriculture, although their efforts at **irrigating** the land were largely unsuccessful. The British seemed more interested in commerce than in the welfare of

KEYWORDS

Irrigate, to supply land with water by means of artificial canals to promote growth of food crops.

Elite, the most powerful or gifted members of a group or community.

Indigenous, native.

the local people. They did little to improve education. They did not address the overwhelming problem of poverty in the country. They were really only interested in what India had to offer them. The British Raj brought Britain to India, adding an **elitist** culture on top of the **indigenous** one. English-only clubs and palaces were built. The British exerted their supremacy over the Indians and treated them as second-class citizens. In chapter 5 we will see how oppressive British legislation would produce shameful moments for India's ruling class and incite demonstrations by the Indians.

The Indians were not happy with the British takeover of their country. More nationalist movements began to emerge. In 1885, a group of lawyers and professionals formed the Indian National Congress, of which Gandhi would later become the leader.

INDEPENDENCE AND PARTITION

By the conclusion of World War II in 1945, Britain had begun talks of independence with the Hindu and Muslim leaders of India. They decided, however, to divide the country up first, because of the continued violence and disruption between Hindus and Muslims. So on August 14 1947, Britain created Pakistan and gave it to the Muslims. On the following day, Britain granted India its independence.

The Victoria Memorial – built by the British as a sign of their prominence in India.

The British have little to be proud of in their conquest of India. They spent over two hundred years in various ways exploiting the people and commerce of the country. The respect with which they began dealings with the Indians depreciated into arrogance and mistreatment. In a country with diverse languages and cultures, Britain imposed its own culture on, requiring English to be the national language, and instead of socializing with the local people, using them as servants.

✱ ✱ ✱ ✱ SUMMARY ✱ ✱ ✱ ✱

- The Mogul dynasty was the last Eastern empire to rule India before its independence.

- The first Europeans to come to India were the Portuguese.

- The East India Company was granted a charter by Elizabeth I in 1600 to begin trading with India.

- In 1757, Warren Hastings, the governor of the East India Company, defeated the Mogul armies in Bengal – from this point the Mogal dynasty declined.

- In 1858 the British decided to take control over all of India – the period of the British Raj.

- In 1876 Queen Victoria was given the title Empress of India. She was never to visit the country.

- In 1885, the Indian National Congress was formed.

- In 1947, India was partitioned creating Pakistan as a Muslim country. India was then given its independence.

Gandhi's Life in South Africa

4

Providence has its appointed hour for everything. We cannot command results, we can only strive.

M.K. Gandhi

As soon as Gandhi stepped off the boat in the eastern port of Natal, he began to notice the disrespectful way that Indians and non-whites were treated in South Africa. Because of this discrimination the Indian population kept to themselves and their dealings with white people were generally limited to business. The majority of Indians in South Africa were labourers. Some of them were **indentured** and some were there as free agents. They were allowed into South Africa on agreements to work for five years at a time. They came to be known as coolies, which was a derogatory umbrella term used for all Indians.

KEYWORDS

Indenture, a deed or sealed agreement between two or more parties.

Turban, a man's headdress worn especially by Hindus, Muslims and Sikhs.

Mohandas began to experience the prejudice and injustice regularly suffered by non-whites. His first culture shock was having to remove his **turban** in court. There was no real reason given for this. It was purely an arbitrary decision. Only Indians in Muslim attire were allowed to keep their turbans on in the presence of the magistrate. The first time he was asked to do so, he refused and left the room. He rebuffed the incident by writing to the papers about the insult and they described him as an 'unwelcome visitor'. Thus, having only just arrived in the country he was already beginning to attract attention and establish a public profile.

PRETORIA

On a trip to Pretoria to argue his first case for his employers, the firm of Dada Abdulla and Company, he encountered further prejudice. His

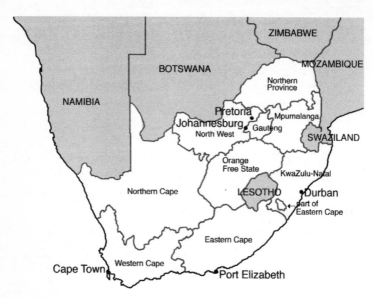

South Africa.

boss, Abdulla Sheth, had procured a first-class ticket for him, so he sat in the first-class compartment of the train. It wasn't long before he was asked to move to third-class accommodation by a train conductor. He refused and the constable was called. He was physically removed from the train and left on the station platform.

During his wait for the next train, he mulled over the idea of returning immediately to India, but he decided to stay and fight for his rights. He sent a long telegram to the General Manager of the railway and to Abdulla Sheth explaining the situation. He did not get any satisfaction from either. Prejudice against Indians was the status quo that people had learned to live with.

MAKING CONTACT WITH OTHER INDIANS

While in Pretoria, Gandhi set about to contact all Indians living there. It was in front of these Indian Merchants that he gave his first public speech. He advised them to form an association that would include all Indian settlers to discuss regularly the racism that they suffered. He also wrote again to the railway authorities to readdress the lack of justification for making first- and second-class ticket holders take third-class provisions if they were not white. The reply that he received was not totally acceptable to him. However, the railway did agree that any 'properly' dressed Indian would be allowed to use such a ticket.

He didn't realize it at the time, but his understanding of the Indian situation in the **Orange Free State** would come in useful at a later date. He stated in his autobiography, 'I saw that South Africa was no country for a self-respecting Indian, and my mind became more and more occupied with the question as to how this state of things might be improved.' He ended up staying a year in Pretoria, and he felt this was the most valuable experience of his life.

KEYWORD

Orange Free State, a state in South Africa in the north of the country.

SETTLING HIS FIRST CASE

Gandhi's first court case in Pretoria and his experiences there set the stage for all his future negotiations. One of his main intentions was to meet with the prosecuting party to establish a relationship with him. He wanted to get to know him as a person. He felt the more he knew of the person as a character and what his circumstance was, the more chance he would have of persuading the two parties to settle out of court. This way both parties would save face. He not only got both parties to refer their case to an arbitrator, he was also able to get them to agree on an outcome that would not financially or socially cripple the loser. As he recalled in his autobiography: 'I had learnt to find out the better side of human nature and to enter men's hearts. I realised that the true function of a lawyer was to unite parties riven asunder.' He spent the better part the next twenty years as a lawyer trying to do just this – orchestrating private compromises.

A FAREWELL PARTY THAT DIDN'T HAPPEN

After Gandhi's court case was finished, he went back to Durban to prepare for his return home to India. At his going away party, a conversation was started about a new law which was to effect all

Indians in South Africa. It was a bill calling for the exemption of Indians in electing members to the Natal Legislative Assembly. This was an important bill because the province of Natal was where the largest concentration of Indians lived. Keeping them from having a voice in the government there would greatly affect their lives. Some of the guests suggested that Gandhi should stay and help them fight for Indian rights. He agreed and his farewell party became a 'working committee' which turned into a new organization for Indian's rights.

THE NATAL INDIAN CONGRESS

Gandhi's practice as a lawyer took a back seat to his public work. He quickly set about gathering 10,000 signatures of Indians in just one fortnight and on the 22 May 1855, the Natal Indian Congress came into being. All members had to pay a subscription to belong to the Congress. Those who earned more money were asked to make larger donations. The Congress operated to serve all Indians by keeping them in touch with each other, promoting debate and providing an outlet for their needs and grievances. It also existed to disseminate information and widely circulated pamphlets containing facts and figures relevant to Indians in South Africa.

The Congress' first test was to challenge a poll tax. It was to be levied against all indentured Indians who wanted to become free agents. Originally, the Government wanted an astounding £25 to be paid annually for this privilege. As Gandhi and his Congress went to work on the tax, the Government reduced it to £3. Gandhi and his supporters were not able to abolish this tax entirely at this time, but the same issue arose again later in his career with positive consequences.

BRIEFLY BACK TO INDIA

Realizing that his commitment in South Africa was going to last for some time, Gandhi sailed back to India in 1896 to collect his family. While in India, he travelled the country to learn of the situation there. He also attended his first meeting of the Indian Congress. By this time he had become less shy and was able to give an impromptu speech.

AN UNWELCOME RETURN

When Gandhi landed back in South Africa, all the passengers on his ship were put into **quarantine** because of their nationality. The Natal Government was trying to intimidate them into returning to India. Gandhi was charged with: **defaming** Natal whites while in India, and bringing in a large quantity of Indians flooding immigration of them in South Africa.

KEYWORDS

Quarantine, a period of isolation and detention.

Defame, attack the good name or reputation of someone or something.

It took Gandhi a while to refute the claims. He was innocent of both, but it still took the government 23 days to decide to let all the passengers go ashore.

PARTICIPATION IN THE BOER WARS

South Africa had suffered a long-standing struggle between the British and the Dutch (at the time called Boers). Both wanted to annex South Africa for their respective countries. The first time they fought each other for supremacy was in the First Boer War in 1877. The Dutch held onto their power and defeated the British at this time, but the conflict rose again, and between 1899 and 1902 the British and Dutch were fighting once more for control over the Orange Free State and the South African Republic region (later to be called the Transvaal). This time the British were the victors. In 1902, a treaty was signed with the Boers and the two defeated Boer republics became British colonies.

Because Gandhi considered himself a loyal subject of the British, he wanted to help when the Boer War started in 1899. However, he wanted to help in a way that did not compromise his principles of non-violence, so he organized an ambulance corps that would be staffed by Indians. His contribution was much appreciated and his ambulance corps raised the prestige of Indians in South Africa. He and his leaders were awarded medals for their service.

SETTING UP PHOENIX

As part of Gandhi's plan to live his life as simply and naturally as possible, he founded an **ashram** in 1904 called Phoenix. This was the first of a number of ashrams that he was to establish. His idea was that anyone who wished

KEYWORD

Ashram, a spiritual community living circumstance.

to live there could do so, regardless of race, creed or colour. But the focus of ashram life was to be politics, hygiene and spirituality.

The rules of the ashram were strict. Each person had to take a vow of:

* truth (this wasn't just about not lying, but included not deceiving people);
* non-violence (this included not being angry with an aggressor);
* celibacy (this included no sexual relations with one's spouse);
* non-possession (this included only owning what was necessary for the nourishment and protection of the body);
* non-stealing (this included only keeping the necessary food needed for use each day);
* fearlessness;
* Swadeshi (wearing only simple clothing without adorning oneself with jewellery etc).

Gandhi structured the daily operations of the ashram to include everyone in manual labour for a good portion of each day. He felt that all residents should participate in the practical upkeep and running of the ashram no matter what their age, service or talents. He included the children in this daily routine as well because he felt it was an important learning process for them. Sometimes their formal education suffered because of his focus on practicalities. In fact later in his life, Gandhi's sons – in particular the eldest – Harilal, felt very strongly that they had been disadvantaged because of Gandhi's lack of attention to their formal schooling.

Gandhi had already started a regular newspaper called *Indian Opinion*, whose production he moved to the Phoenix farm. One of the first tasks of the residents of Phoenix was to decide how they were going to continue to produce the newspaper on time alongside getting their community up and running, building houses, etc.

VOW OF BRAHMACHARYA

As Mohandas matured he was starting to consider the idea of becoming a celibate renunciate. He felt that in order to do his public work he had to tightly control his personal desires and habits. He also felt that redirecting his energies was vital for a man who was seeking God. This was not an idea that he came to or acted on quickly. For Mohandas a vow was serious and final and one didn't go back on it. For this reason he did not take the vow of brahmacharya (celibacy) until he felt that he was ready to give his life to it.

THE BLACK LAW AND HIS FIRST ARREST

During this time, the British Government in South Africa declared a new statute called the Black Law. This meant that all Indians would have to register with their local authority and have their fingerprints taken. Anyone not complying with the legislation would be fined, imprisoned or deported. Of course, Gandhi vowed to fight this law and assembled three thousand Indians in Johannesburg to discuss it.

Gandhi felt his only option was to refuse to register and he was promptly arrested. At that point, General Jan Smuts (1870–1950), the president of the Transvaal, told Gandhi if the Indians would voluntarily register the law would be repealed. Gandhi convinced many Indians to register, but Smuts went back on his word. Gandhi was beaten up by a number of angry Indians who felt they had been mislead by him. To show that he did not know about this treachery, he convinced the Indians to burn their new registration cards. Gandhi was arrested again.

FIGHTING FOR INDIAN RIGHTS IN ENGLAND

Between 1906 and 1909 Mohandas travelled twice to England to help publicize the plight of Indians in South Africa. His trip in 1909 was eye opening for him. He became very aware of the **extremism** that existed not only in England, but in the Western world as a whole.

KEYWORD

Extremism, supporting fanatical or radical political opinions.

He felt that modern civilization had completely divorced man from his natural surroundings and spiritual nature. He thought that medicine and science had pitted man against nature and bound him to scientific materialism.

Gandhi felt that the difficulties in the world arose not because of conflicts between people, but the differences in their cultures. He felt that the British had tainted the culture of South Africa with the selfish and materialistic way in which Westerners lived their lives. This observation would lead him to write one of his most famous documents called *Hind Swaraj* which became his manifesto for independence for India.

LAST FEW YEARS IN SOUTH AFRICA

When Gandhi returned to South Africa, he would stay only for a short time before returning to his homeland for good. He continued his work for the Indian population there and was arrested more than once for his protests.

One of the laws that he rebelled against was that of the illegality of Indian marriages. South African legislation ruled that only Christian marriages were recognized by the State. This meant that Hindus, Muslims and Parsees found their marriages non-existent in the eyes of the law and their children were therefore illegitimate.

Through Gandhi's persistence, his knowledge of the law and his ability to organize, he helped the oppressed Indians of South Africa unite and stand up for themselves. He taught them that they did not have to put up with prejudice and they could demand their rights if they were organized. He did a great deal for their confidence as a people. On 30 June 1914, Gandhi signed a pact with General Jan Smuts. The agreement was a compromise between what the State had originally intended to keep as law and what Gandhi demanded for the Indians. Their historical pact recognized the dignity of the Indian people, the validity of their marriages and the abolishment of tax on indentured workers. In return, the Indian population was to agree not to travel between the different states of South Africa without carrying an identification card. With this agreement in place, Gandhi felt it was time to return to his homeland.

✳ ✳ ✳ ✳ *SUMMARY* ✳ ✳ ✳ ✳

- As soon as Mohandas set foot in South Africa he began to notice the disrespect with which all (non-whites) were treated.

- Gandhi began to organize the Indian population in South Africa.

- In a court case in Pretoria, he managed to convince both defendant and plaintiff to settle out of court, thus saving face for both and avoiding social and financial ruin for the loser.

- In 1896, Mohandas returned to India for a year to collect his family.

- Upon his arrival back in South Africa he was charged with trying to flood Natal with Indian immigrants and defaming white South Africans while in India.

- He created an ambulance corps made up of Indians to serve in the Boer War and was awarded a medal for his efforts.

- In 1903 he produced a pamphlet for Indian rights called *Indian Opinion*.

- In 1904 he set up his first ashram called Phoenix.

- In 1906, he took a vow of brahmacharya (celibacy).

- Gandhi travelled to England in 1906 and 1909 to help publicize the fight for rights of Indians in South Africa. En route to England in 1909 he wrote his manifesto for Indian home rule called *Hind Swaraj*.

- In 1914 he orchestrated an agreement with General Smuts to recognize Indian rights, marriages and the abolition of indentured tax. He then left South Africa for good.

5 Firmness in Truth – 'Satyagraha'

*Non-violence is the greatest force at the disposal
of mankind. It is mightier than the mightiest weapon
of destruction devised by the ingenuity of man.*

M.K. Gandhi

Aside from prolonged fasting as a means of campaigning for justice, Gandhi is probably most remembered for his development of the concept of satyagraha, which means 'firmness in truth' or 'the force of truth'. It is more than a concept, it was also the name that he gave to his supporters and the crusades he initiated. He was looking for a phrase that would be their calling card and would represent their cause for justice, Indian rights and the passively resistant way they intended to proceed.

The phrase satyagraha was originally 'sadagraha', coined by one of Gandhi's cousins during the three thousand strong meeting in Johannesburg mentioned in the previous chapter. Sadagraha means 'steadfastness in a good cause' but Gandhi altered it slightly to add the concept of 'ahimsa' or 'non-killing' to it. He borrowed the concept of ahimsa from the Jain tradition and it would become a pivotal theory from which all of his movements were based.

The philosophy behind the phrase formed the core of all of the work that Gandhi would do. It framed his entire existence and relationship with people. It included turning the other cheek, helping one's enemy in times of need, patience and never losing one's composure to anger. It also included respecting all living beings and treating everyone as one would like to be treated oneself. His social reforms philosophy applied equally to his personal life. As with many leaders, his personal and private lives were entwined.

Gandhi as a young adult.

RETURN TO INDIA

Gandhi was received back in India with such a welcome it over-whelmed him. His skirmishes with the Government of South Africa had made him famous. He had attracted international attention in his satyagraha movements. Although he had a reputation that preceded him, he took the advice of a friend and initially refrained from starting any commotion in India. He took two years to travel the country and understand the situation within his homeland first.

He always travelled in third-class compartments and was appalled by the filth and rudeness that he experienced there. Hygiene was something to which Gandhi felt everyone should aspire, whether or not they were educated. He saw it as a form of self-respect and of homage to God. This had been one of his quests in his first ashram and it would continue to be a reform that he would try to create in India as well.

During his travels he was asked by the governor of Bombay, Willingdon (later the viceroy Lord Willingdon), to meet with him. Willingdon asked Gandhi to come to him first, whatever ideas he had pertaining to the British Government in India. Gandhi agreed to this promise.

Later on in his dealings with Gandhi, when Willingdon became the viceroy, he was quoted in Brown's biography, *Gandhi, Prisoner of Hope* (see Further Reading), as saying to the Secretary of State about Gandhi:

'You will find him I think amenable and anxious to help, with a real desire to work out a satisfactory constitution. I do not think you will find him in any way a violent extremist, or that he will be likely to walk out in order to create a demonstration. I must confess to a sense of extreme relief at having got rid of the little man for a few short months, for while we are the best of friends, he certainly is the most difficult man to pin down in the matter of negotiations. He may be a saint, he may be a holy man; he is I believe quite sincere in his principles; but of this I am perfectly certain, that he is one of the most astute, politically-minded and bargaining little gentlemen I ever came across...Still I feel that he will be a help and not a hindrance.'

BECOMING MAHATMA

From his birth, Gandhi was known as Mohandas, but a friendship with Rabindranath Tagore (1861–1941), a well-known poet and high-ranking Bengal mystic, would change the way people addressed him for generations to come. Gandhi met Tagore in his travels around India. He purposely went to a school that Tagore had set up to meet this man whom he revered.

Tagore and Gandhi were in awe of each other, although they had very different approaches to life. Gandhi strove for the simplest of lifestyles. He encouraged everyone to participate more in the practical details of life, such as cooking, cleaning etc, feeling it was as important as intellectual pursuits. Tagore, on the other hand, was an idealist who was not opposed to the indulgences of a more Western culture.

Once at Tagore's school, Gandhi tried to introduce the reforms that he was promoting. While he was there, Tagore allowed him make changes in the students' daily routines. But after Gandhi left, Tagore let the school return to its previous mode of operation. In the meantime, both Gandhi and Tagore began to address each other with new names. Gandhi called Tagore 'Great Sentinel' and Tagore christened Gandhi 'Great Soul', or Mahatma. Hence this title became the most popularly used name for Gandhi for the rest of his life.

SIMPLIFYING HIS DRESS USING THE SPINNING WHEEL

By this time Gandhi had long since given up wearing his Western dress and had developed an outfit that he felt exemplified satyagraha. It was made of Indian cloth and was very simple. As he described it in his autobiography: 'I had altered my dress so as to make it more in keeping with that of the indentured labourers, ...consisting of a shirt, a **dhoti**, a cloak and a

KEYWORDS

Dhoti, men's wrap-around trousers.

Swardeshi, using only indigenous goods and materials.

white scarf, all made of Indian mill cloth.' He required all of his ashramites to wear the same attire. It became another outward expression of his concepts of **swardeshi** and nationalism.

The simple spinning of cloth became another important symbol of Gandhi's offensives and philosophy. He spun each day himself for a few hours. He found this the most enjoyable time of his day because he said that it gave him time to ponder.

By spinning he was also putting into practice what he asserted to others. He believed that Indians should take pride in their own resources and thus make their clothes from indigenous materials. The spinning that he and his followers did was also used to promote Indian cotton for Indian use and thereby reject British goods. He only wore material that he had spun himself from native cotton and he expected his followers to do the same.

FREE INDIA MANIFESTO

During Gandhi's trip to England in 1909, to promote the plight of Indians in South Africa, he came up with the concept of home rule for India. The idea came about from his experiences of racism towards Indians in South Africa, his home country and the keen disappointment he felt at seeing the British Government's apparent apathy towards abolishing it there or in India. He created a new publication called *Hind Swaraj* in which he wrote his famous **manifesto** to free India from British rule.

> **KEYWORD**
>
> Manifesto, a public declaration of intent, policy, aims etc.
>
> Untouchables, the lowest of Hindu social classes.

The format for the pamphlet was questions from the reader and answers from the editor (namely Gandhi). His basic premise was that only people who can rule themselves can control themselves, and that people without freedom cannot command respect. In his manifesto he didn't just promote resistance to the British rule in India, but he made a calling for Indians to reform themselves as well. The main changes that Gandhi felt needed to be made by his fellow countrymen were tolerance and cooperation of all religions, the abolishment of the social stigma of the **Untouchables** and an increased sense of nationalism.

RELIGION AND POLITICS

Gandhi considered himself a very religious man. He also felt his 21 years of experience in South Africa had shown him his true calling in life. He felt compelled to organize the Indian people to take responsibility for their circumstances and to develop self-respect. He felt that politics were not separate from what he was trying to achieve spiritually and that a truly religious person could not disassociate himself from politics. His religious concepts formed the core of his behaviour and that of his satyagraha movements. In fact he designed his local satyagraha campaigns for the wider involvement of people in politics. His inspiration for politics is described Brown's biography, *Gandhi, Prisoner of Hope*: '...a man who aspires after that cannot afford to keep out of any field of life. That is why my devotion to Truth has drawn me into the field of politics; and I can say without the slightest hesitation, and yet in all humility, that those who say that religion has nothing to do with politics do not know what religion means.'

WORK WITH THE UNTOUCHABLES

One of Gandhi's life-long commitments was the abolishment of the Untouchable caste. The Untouchables are a religious and cultural designation. As mentioned in Chapters 1 and 2, in Hindu tradition, each person is born into a caste and is unable to change their status. Thus, their caste provides the essence of their life's work and associations.

The Untouchables are the lowest caste in Hindu culture. It is their role in life to perform the most base and menial of tasks. They are to be kept separate in all walks of life – they cook their food and eat separately, and other castes are not to look upon them. They are destined to a life of service to members of higher castes and they are thought of as almost less than human. These are the poorest and least educated of the classes in India. When Gandhi let them become a part of his new ashram in Ahemenbad, he received much criticism from within his own culture and created a good deal of controversy. He also met with disagreement on this front with his own wife Kasturbai.

The main benefactor of the ashram threatened to remove his funding if Untouchables were allowed to live there. He contributed a hefty sum to the running costs, and without his money they would be in difficulty. Gandhi, however, felt he needed to stick to his principles and decided to meet the consequences whatever they might be. The patron did remove his support, but fortunately another stepped in with funding to keep the ashram going.

Gandhi did not allow any of these difficulties to prevent him from working tirelessly to demonstrate how he felt the Untouchables should be treated. He cleaned out his own toilet and cut his own hair, which were tasks that had always been left for the Untouchables to do. Gandhi also required his family to follow suit. At first Kasturbai was furious at having to do these things, but because of her faith and respect for her husband, she eventually came to do what he asked of her.

THE INDIGO WORKERS
Back in his home country, one of the first causes that Gandhi investigated was that of the indigo growers in the Champaran region. Champaran is located in the northeastern region of India. It was a very rural and poor area at the time. Essentially, farmers were being exploited heavily by their British landlords. They were forced to set aside a portion of their land for the growing of indigo, which was used by the British for themselves. At harvest, all of the profits from the indigo had to be given to their landlords.

Gandhi met with a crowd of thousands of indigo growers who told him they were ready to go to prison for their cause. With such a large uprising, the governors decided to set up a commission to examine the case. Gandhi demanded that the government require the British planters to give back 50 per cent of their ill-gotten gains to the farmers. The Government offered 25 per cent and Gandhi accepted. It was not the first time that Gandhi settled for a compromise, nor would it be the last. More importantly than the compromise Gandhi was able to establish, the situation had highlighted the enormity of the exploitation of the British.

THE AMRITSAR MASSACRE
The British Government put into effect new laws called the Rowlatt Bills in 1919. The original intention was for them to give the British control over any terrorism while the war was being fought, but after the war the laws were kept in place. The laws would make it possible for anyone to be arrested on the mere suspicion that they might be a subversive. Added to this they could be dealt with without a trial and could be held in prison for up to two years.

Gandhi was appalled at the level of oppression and unfairness of these laws so he organized his satyagraha. He was so successful that most of India was to go on strike, closing shops, not sending children to schools, and participating in mass demonstrations.

It should be noted here, that even though Gandhi's remit was for non-violence, he was not always able to control the huge numbers of people demonstrating in different areas of the country, and it was the case at this time that violence did erupt in some places.

Unfortunately, General Reginald Dyer (1864–1927) was in charge of the operation on the British side. In a walled garden in Amritsar in Punjab, where there were 20,000 demonstrators, he ordered his men to open fire on them. There was nowhere for them to escape to. The army was blocking the only exit. Dyer's men continued to shoot until they had exhausted all their ammunition, killing approximately 400 people.

When Gandhi heard about the violence he immediately suspended the protests, but the massacre had stirred people up and the violence continued for the next few days. Gandhi felt terrible about what happened. He said he had made a mistake of 'Himalayan proportions'.

PARTICIPATION IN THE INDIAN NATIONAL CONGRESS

1920 was an important year for Gandhi. He returned his medals to the British as a declaration of his disappointment with their oppressive rule in India. His influence with the Indian National Congress was mounting. He rallied thousands of people to burn their British-made clothes and the Indian National Congress had adopted the spinning wheel as the symbol for their flag. He became more and more popular with his idea of home rule and he became the unrivalled leader of the Congress.

SIX YEARS IN PRISON

Gandhi's second great anti-British campaign ran from 1920–1922. He wanted to unite Muslims and Hindus for their one great cause – non-cooperation with the British.

In 1922, thousands of people quit their government jobs. People boycotted everything British, their goods, their schools, etc, but once again, the demonstrations stirred up such emotion that violence broke out. A number of policemen in Chauri Chaura were set alight and burnt alive. Gandhi was horrified by the mob rule and suspended the satyagraha movement again. He was arrested again for inciting civil unrest and put in prison in 1922 for six years.

* * * *SUMMARY* * * *

- Gandhi's lifestyle and political campaigns were designed around his idea of satyagraha, meaning 'firmness in truth'.

- His concept of negotiation and civil disobedience included passive resistance and ahimsa, meaning 'non-killing'.

- He was given the name Mahatma meaning 'great soul' by an Indian poet named Tagore.

- He spun every day and made his own clothes, and the spinning wheel became a symbol of his reform movement.

- His concept of Indian home rule also included reforms for his own countrymen of religious tolerance.

- Gandhi spent the greater part of his career trying to remove the stigma and persecution of the Untouchable caste.

- A campaign in against the Rowlatt Bills in 1919 incited a massacre of Indian protestors in Punjab – Gandhi called off the campaign.

- By 1920 Gandhi had become the leader of the Indian National Congress.

- Gandhi's anti-British campaign got out of control in 1922 with the burning alive of several policemen

- In 1922, Gandhi was arrested and sent to prison for six years for inciting civil unrest.

Experiments with Fasting, Dietetics and Health

*The carnal mind, instead of controlling the senses, becomes
their slave, and therefore the body always needs clean
non-stimulating foods and periodical fasting.*

M.K. Gandhi

Gandhi was interested in life as a **holistic**
process. He observed that everything in life
was intertwined. He knew that what a person
ate, the state of their health, their patterns of
behaviours and their thoughts were inexorably

KEYWORD

Holistic, body, mind and
spirit.

linked. He realized that in order to address and change any one of these
aspects, one had to probe them all. He believed that reforms needed to
start at home with the individual before addressing the wider
community.

He exemplified this in his life. Anything that he proposed for the
community or country, he had already privately committed himself to
and was already doing. He experimented with many concepts and
behaviours. His religious background was the cornerstone for much of
his thinking and actions.

Gandhi spent a great deal of time refining his own diet and eventually
he lived mainly on fresh and sun-dried fruits, nuts, seeds and goat's
milk. By the time he was in his forties he had made a vow to himself
never to eat more than five items of food in one 24-hour period, and
never to eat after sunset.

HYGIENE

One of the Mahatma's health focuses was on hygiene. Poor and uneducated Indians had a reputation for being slovenly and not keeping their houses or environment clean. This was one of the blemishes on his people that he hoped to eradicate. He also wished to help eradicate the threat of disease by teaching people about good hygiene.

He was appalled by the squalor that people allowed themselves to live in. He didn't feel it mattered whether a person was poor, there was still plenty that could be done to make their lives healthier, simply by applying some discipline to their hygiene. He knew that many people didn't have the money to help themselves, for example, to buy another set of clothes so they could wash the ones they were wearing, but he felt that if they were inspired and cooperated together, there was much they could do. Whenever Gandhi travelled, whether in South Africa or India, he talked to the villagers about simple hygiene.

HIS SON'S SICKNESS

Gandhi was enamoured with children. He loved having them around. He loved taking care of them and was very maternal with them. He had five children altogether, all sons. The first child, however, died at birth. Although he was busy fighting considerable public issues, he assumed primary responsibility for the direction of his children's upbringing, education and health. He assisted at the delivery of his last child, and when they were

KEYWORDS

Typhoid, acute infectious disease characterized by fever, skin rash and headache.

Pneumonia, inflammation of one or both lungs in which the air sacs become filled with liquid.

ill, he also shared in their care. Gandhi also took over the nursing of his eldest son when he became ill with **typhoid** and **pneumonia**. A doctor, who advised many other Hindu families, recommended that his son be given eggs and chicken broth. Gandhi wouldn't hear of it. He recounts in his autobiography telling the doctor: 'To my mind it is only on such occasions, that a man's faith is truly tested. Rightly or wrongly it is part of my religious conviction that man may not eat meat, eggs, and the like...I must therefore take the risk that you say is likely.' The doctor refused to treat his son if he was not able to prescribe what he felt was the best treatment, and released him from his care.

KEYWORDS

Homoeopathy, the treatment of disease by minute doses of drugs that in a healthy person would produce symptoms of the disease.

Hydropathic, method of treating illness using water.

As Gandhi was nursing his son with his **hydropathic** treatment and a juice fast, his condition worsened. He became heavy with fever and delirium. Gandhi was afraid for his life. He also feared that others would think him an irresponsible parent. He left his son and went for a walk praying as he went along. When he returned, his son was out of danger. His fever had resided and he was on the road to recovery. Gandhi said he didn't know whether his son's recovery was due to God's grace, the hydropathy, or to his nursing skills, but he felt unequivocally that God had saved his honour that day.

KASTURBAI'S ILLNESS

There were other times in Gandhi's life and that of his family, when their faith in **homeopathic** and natural medicine were put to the test. Both he and his wife had a few serious ailments which could have killed them. Throughout their ordeals, both held firm in their belief in using only natural and vegetarian remedies.

While they were living in South Africa, Kasturbai began to haemorrhage. After much debate she finally agreed to have surgery because it was the only thing that could cure her. A few days later she developed complications. The doctor wanted to give her meat broth because she was so weak. Gandhi refused. The doctor told him he would not be responsible for his wife's health anymore if he did not agree to let him give what he felt was the right treatment. Gandhi consulted with his wife as to her wishes. She told him that she would not take the broth, so Gandhi took his wife home and began to nurse her himself.

He had some grave doubts about whether or not he was doing the right thing, but Kasturbai assured him that nothing was going to happen to her. He set about giving her hydropathic treatments and feeding her milk. She recovered and their resolve to follow their personal convictions was even more secured.

HIS OWN ILLNESSES

Gandhi himself suffered a number of illnesses including a bout with malaria. He was a very slight man, only 5'5" in height and weighing around 8 stone, so any significant weight loss during illness could have put him in serious danger.

During World War I, Gandhi was committed to helping recruit men to fight for the British. This put a great deal of strain on him. At the time his diet consisted mainly of nut butters and lemons. He recognized later on that he could have seriously damaged his health on such a restricted and purifying diet.

During this time he had a very bad case of dysentery that he couldn't recover from. He also had a constant fever. He refused medical aid and tried hydrotherapy but he was not getting any better. He entrusted his care to an unconventional doctor named Talvalkar who applied ice all over his body. Although Gandhi was not convinced of the validity of this treatment, he did start to improve. He was then given injections of arsenic by another aryurvedic doctor who encouraged him to eat eggs or milk. Gandhi had long since taken a vow never to use either. But Kasturbai, upon hearing him report this to the doctor, suggested that goat's milk would not be the same as cow's milk. Because Gandhi knew he was close to death, he decided to try goat's milk, which he would continue to use for the rest of his life. He never fully resolved the conflict in his mind about using the milk, even though he knew he needed it to rebuild and maintain his health.

FASTING FOR SPIRITUAL HEALTH

A considerable part of Gandhi's investigation into fasting was connected to his beliefs about self-restraint, and not purely a health issue. He felt that denying oneself comforts was a sign of virtue. He observed that denial helped to train the body and the mind, making one more receptive to the life force of the Divine. He was continually trying to gain mastery over his body so his attention could be freed up for devotion to God. It is important to remember that he felt that politics and religion were not divorced from one other, so his political accomplishments were also seen as his spiritual successes and his work within the greater community was representative of his relationship with God. He needed to be an example to others, which is one reason he never wavered in his vows.

Gandhi observed that fasting seemed to suppress one's carnal desires. This was of great interest to the Mahatma because he struggled throughout his life with his sexuality. His experiments with dietetics demonstrated to him that certain foods increased one's lustful desires, but fasting, in particular, took them away. So fasting, for him also became a tool for avoiding sexual arousal.

Gandhi also used fasting as a way to do penance for the wrong-doing and shortcomings of others. He felt responsible as a leader of people. If, under his direction, people fell short of his expectations, he maintained that it was up to him to atone for their failings.

In his publication *Young India* which he produced between 1924–26 he gave this advice for those wanting to experiment with fasting. He said that anyone should fast if they:

* are constipated;
* are anaemic;
* are feverish;
* have a headache;

* have digestion problems;
* are rheumatic;
* are depressed or fretting.

He believed that people should only eat when they were hungry and after they had laboured for their food.

His recommendations for what to do when engaging in a fast were:

* Conserve mental and physical energy throughout the fast.
* Do not think about food.
* Drink plenty of cold water with or without soda or salt.
* Have a warm sponge bath daily – preferably in the morning sun.
* Take regular enemas throughout the fast.
* Sleep in the open air as much as possible.
* Keep your attention on your relationship with God.

FASTING AS A POLITICAL TOOL

Gandhi was perhaps the first person ever to use fasting as a political strategy. In his public life he undertook 17 major fasts for political reasons. The first time he used fasting publicly was to express his protest for the treatment of Indians in South Africa in 1913.

Probably his most famous fasts took place in Calcutta in 1947 and 1948. Both of these he accepted to be 'to the death' unless there was some resolve to the Hindu–Muslim violence that was ravaging the country. His fasting attracted international attention and concern and people all over the world kept abreast of his physical status. It was such a serious gesture to put one's own life on the line for others, but people's condolences or visits were not enough – he required resolutions in writing before he would ever stop a fast.

Five out of his 17 public fasts took place while he was in prison. At the age of 78, Gandhi began what was to be his last fast on 13 January,

1948. It was in response to rioting that had broken out in Calcutta, one of India's largest cities.

He was quoted in Clement's biography, *Father of a Nation* (see Further Reading), as saying during his last fast: 'Death for me would be a glorious deliverance rather than that I should be a helpless witness of the destruction of India, Hinduism, Sikhism and Islam...I am in God's hands.'

The Mahatma was determined to fast until the disturbances had ceased. He was never able to know the results of the conflict because he was assassinated 12 days into the fast.

✳✳✳✳SUMMARY✳✳✳✳

- Gandhi saw life as a holistic process.

- He experimented throughout his life with dietary and health practices to purify the body and mind.

- One of his main health focuses was hygiene.

- He loved children and was very involved in their care and upbringing.

- He took charge of nursing his son's broken arm and another son who was ill with typhoid.

- He nursed his wife through a severe illness with hydropathic treatments and milk.

- He refused conventional medical treatment whenever he was sick.

- He used fasting privately as a means of physical and spiritual purification, and publicly as a means of protest.

7 The Salt March Led by the 'Half-naked Fakir'

One must be the change one wishes to see in the world.

M.K. Gandhi

Before going into the details of what was perhaps Gandhi's most famous demonstration of non-cooperation, it would be useful to look at the background leading up to this historical protest.

While Gandhi was serving time in jail in the 1920s, he started to write his autobiography *The Story of My Experiments with Truth*. The book only covers his life up until around 1921, for two reasons. Firstly, he felt that most of his life had already been so well documented. From that year on, that there was no need for him to write about those events as well. Secondly, his life was becoming so complicated in terms of all the people and explanations he would have to include that he decided to limit the book. He was not completely enthusiastic about writing his autobiography in the first place and only did so at the urging of his colleagues. He was more interested in fighting his causes than writing an account of them.

While he was in prison in the 1920s the situation was heating up politically speaking on the outside. There was a large division in the Indian National Congress, and the conflicts between Muslims and Hindus continued to erupt into violence. The Indian Natal Congress was divided. Some members wanted India to be partitioned so that Muslims and Hindus would have their own countries to live in. Others held Mahatma Gandhi's viewpoint that they should try to live together. He felt that it would be a terrible mistake to divide the country because he believed that learning to live peacefully together was the solution for India's future.

One of Gandhi's staunch supporters was Jawaharlal Nehru (1889–1964) who would later become the Prime Minister of India. He also spent time in and out of jail as a participant in Gandhi's satyagraha campaigns. He was in jail with the Mahatma following the violence at Chauri Chaura, as described in chapter 5.

GIVING UP LEADERSHIP OF THE CONGRESS

When Gandhi and Nehru were released from prison in 1924, Gandhi suggested to the Congress that Nehru take over as their leader. Nehru did eventually take over as Gandhi's successor but not until 1934. Gandhi wanted to move to the background in politics and instead focus his campaigns at the grass roots level. He wanted to participate in the practicalities of local people's lives.

Gandhi took again to travelling throughout India. His aim was to spend his time reforming India from the inside out. He was dedicated to cleaning up people's environments and making them hygenically healthy places to live. He used his energies to educate the poor about health and well being. He also founded a spinner's association in keeping with his swadeshi concept, and he spoke out as an advocate for women's rights.

A YEAR OF MEDITATION

In 1926, Gandhi decided to spend the entire year in meditation. He would only allow his silence to be broken on very rare occasions. He so liked the idea of being economical with his speech that after his year of silence he started a discipline for himself of spending one day a week in total silence. Every Monday he refused to be drawn into conversation for the entire day.

When he finished his year of silence he had three priorities he wanted to address in the greater population:

1 The dissolution of child marriages.
2 The protection of the cow as a sacred animal for Hindus.
3 The promotion of the Indian national language instead of English.

REINSTATING THE SATYAGRAHA MOVEMENT

Gandhi had suspended his last satyagraha movement in 1922 after violence had broken out because of it, but he was now ready to re-enter politics and start up the campaign again.

To do this, he went to Bardoli which is where he was when he suspended the movement. In 1928, inspired by Gandhi, 87,000 local residents stood firm against the newest tax levy. Their taxes were to go up an astonishing 22 per cent. They were committed to this act of civil disobedience and were willing to go to jail for their opposition. To try and break their resolve, the Government confiscated their land, livestock and possessions, but the residents held firm.

The authorities finally gave in and returned everything they had seized. Though Gandhi made no headway with abolishing the tax, the Government returned it to its original levels. This slow but steady progress was something Gandhi had the patience to endure, however, not everyone was capable of waiting for significant results.

IMPATIENCE WITH THE NON-VIOLENCE POLICY

Gandhi had aroused the feelings of an entire nation, but it was not an easy task to keep the momentum going, let alone get everyone to agree on how things were to proceed. The people felt they were being exploited by the British. They were treated as second-class citizens in their own country, and they had lost some of their national identity. As well as the anti-British feelings, there was still a great division between Hindus and Muslims.

During a meeting of the Indian National Congress, some of the younger members grew very impatient with Gandhi's slow progress. They demanded that the Congress announce that India was taking its independence immediately. Gandhi managed to convince them to wait one more year to give the British Raj a chance to come to this conclusion themselves. The Raj made no such acknowledgment during this time.

While people waited for something definitive to happen, terrorism was rife. In desperation the viceroy, Lord Irwin, tried to set up a round table conference. He thought India should become a **dominion**, but the conference did not take place until 1931. In 1930, Gandhi, pressured by his followers, publicly announced

> **KEYWORD**
>
> Dominion, the name formerly given to a self-ruling division of the British empire.

that India was independent. This declaration of independence represented more of a psychological change than a practical one. India was still occupied by a foreign nation. Nothing had changed by the declaration other than a revival of India's national identity.

THE MARCH FROM AHMEDABAD TO DANDI

In the midst of this tense time, Gandhi told the Government that he was organizing another protest. He declared that one would take place in nine days, although at the time of his announcement, he didn't know what he was going to do.

Gandhi set off from his ashram near Ahmedabad to walk the 230 miles to Dandi. He started his walk with about 70 residents from his ashram. It took two and a half months to reach the coast line, and he picked up thousands of people along the way. Many people stopped what they were doing and left their villages to join Gandhi on his epic walk. The Mahatma was now 61 years old and the oldest member of the protest group.

As he walked, Gandhi proposed that people disregard the salt laws which prohibited them from harvesting from the sea themselves. The British had a monopoly on all salt and it was illegal to extract any for personal use and sell it. Gandhi headed straight for the coast where salt would be lying washed up on the shore, and he intended to be photographed collecting it.

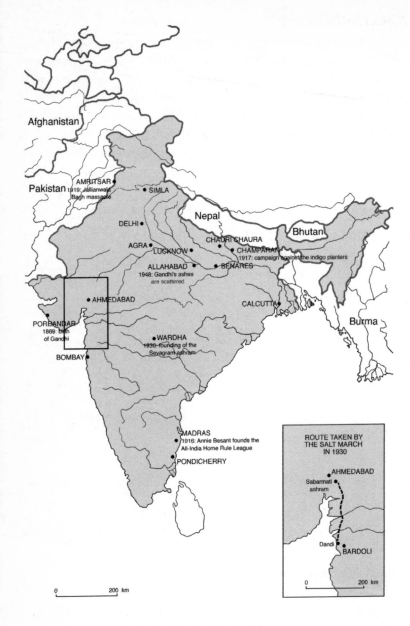

India. (Inset: route taken by the Salt March in 1930.)

WORLDWIDE PUBLICITY

It is not immediately obvious to see the connection between the salt laws and the struggle for India's independence, which was Gandhi's ultimate goal. This was part of the uniqueness and eccentricity of the Mahatma. He persevered to make a point wherever he could, particularly if it helped unite the Indian people and give them confidence. Gandhi, while keeping his eye on the bigger picture, was always trying to work things from the ground up.

As was the case over the years, Gandhi attracted much international interest. During his salt march, he had the time to accumulate photographers and journalists from around the world to watch and report the event.

When Gandhi reached the shores of the Indian Ocean, he reached down and picked up a handful of salt. His first handful of salt was auctioned off to the highest bidder.

The Mahatma had created mayhem. All over the country people were gathering salt. They also began selling it in their local village markets which was completely forbidden. Approximately 75,000 Indians were arrested and hundreds killed in violent clashes with the police. Gandhi was arrested within a month and found himself back in jail. He was initially pleased to be there because he felt he could get some rest, but that was not going to happen.

THE DELHI PACT

While Gandhi was in jail this time, the situation between the Hindus and Muslims began raging again. Lord Irwin was not happy that Gandhi was back in jail. He needed him to help with negotiations. Irwin visited Gandhi in prison to start a dialogue.

Irwin and Gandhi came to an agreement which was called the Delhi Pact. The compromise that they agreed was for Gandhi to call off his movement of civil disobedience, and in return thousands of Indians would be released. The agreement also allowed people in the coastal areas to gather small amounts of salt for themselves, and included the right of Indians to **boycott** British textiles.

Irwin released Gandhi from prison so that he could be present at what would finally be the first Round Table Conference, which was to take place in London in August 1930. The agenda of the conference was not India's independence, but the situation between the Hindus and the Muslims. The situation of Hindu–Muslim unity was always one of monumental importance for Gandhi. The unification of the Hindu and Muslim people was something he considered had to go hand in hand in order for India to gain its independence and he knew it would be one of his greatest challenges. He stated in his autobiography: 'I had realized early enough in South Africa that there was no genuine friendship between the Hindus and the Musalmans. I never missed an opportunity to remove obstacles in the way of unity. It was not in my nature to placate anyone by adulation, or at the cost of self-respect. But my South African experiences had convinced me that it would be on the question of Hindu–Muslim unity that my Ahimsa would be put to its severest test, and that the question presented the widest field for my experiments in Ahimsa.'

GANDHI WINS THE HEARTS OF MANY ENGLISH PEOPLE

While he was in England, Gandhi and his entourage stayed in a poor area in the East End. He refused the accommodation in a hotel that was offered to him. Now whenever he travelled, Gandhi always bought the lowest class tickets and lived among the poorest of the people. He was always making a point by doing this.

The media in England loved him and delighted in following him around. He toured around the country from September until December. He visited factory workers, students, professors and members of Parliament. He was received at court by George V (1865–1936) at Buckingham Palace. Wherever he went people came out to meet and greet him, but Gandhi was most concerned with meeting the people who were against the liberation of India. In particular, one person he very much wanted to meet was Winston Churchill (1874–1965). Churchill disliked Gandhi with a vengeance and never met with him. He famously described Gandhi as a 'semi-naked **fakir** whose idea of treating the king and the viceroy as equals was nauseating'. He is also quoted as saying in *Gandhi Father of a Nation*: 'I have not become the King's first minister in order to preside at the liquidation of the British Empire.'

ROUND TABLE CONFERENCE

The conference was quite substantial and included representatives from all the religious and social strata of India: the business world, the Untouchables, the Muslims, Christians and Hindus. Gandhi had gone to England with high hopes for some much needed reforms. He was sorely disappointed the conference was a failure.

Part of the problem was that the English wanted to keep the separate factions in India polarized, and they did their best to further this end by pitting them against each other. It was their idea of 'divide and conquer'. The British were not ready to release India to home rule. They felt it was more than they could give up. They reduced the conference to talking about minor points, so Gandhi was no closer to home rule by the end of the conference than when he left India.

THE 'KING AND EMPEROR'S HOSPITALITY'

Very disappointed with the results of the congress, Gandhi went back to India.

He had hardly been back in India a month when he was arrested again for inciting civil unrest and this time sent to prison for 15 months. This would be his fourth visit to enjoy 'the King and Emperor's hospitality' as he called it.

As was mentioned earlier, Gandhi enjoyed going to prison. He loved the statement it made about sticking to one's beliefs. For him it was also a time of reflection a time to create new strategies and a time to rest. He did not usually have time for reading, so he used his time in prison to catch up. He was a voracious reader and read everything from politics and religion to fiction.

In many ways, Gandhi was just as vivid a leader behind bars as he was when free. He wrote a great deal while in prison so he could keep his followers updated on his views.

✳ ✳ ✳ ✳ SUMMARY ✳ ✳ ✳ ✳

- Gandhi began writing his auto-biography while in prison – he called it *My Experiments with Truth.*

- Gandhi travelled around the country working with people and trying to educate them about hygiene and healthy living.

- In 1926 Gandhi began a year of silence and meditation. When he finished his year, he began to focus on:

  1) The abolition of child marriages.
  2) The protection of the cow as a sacred animal for Hindus.
  3) The promotion of the Indian national language instead of English.

- Many of Gandhi's followers were impatient with the slowness of his progress and instigated violence.

- On 12 March 1930, Gandhi began a protest march against the monopoly the British had on the gathering and selling of salt.

- Viceroy Lord Irwin, visited Gandhi in jail to negotiate. Their compromise was called the Delhi Pact.

- Gandhi was released from prison to attend the Round Table Conference in London which was a dismal failure.

- His very presence irritated Churchill who called him a 'half-naked fakir'.

- He was as vivid a leader behind bars as he was when he was free.

The Road to Independence 8

*Freedom is never dear at any price, it is the breath of life.
What would a man not pay for living?*

M.K. Gandhi

To understand how a single person could make such a sweeping impact on an entire country, one needs to look at the small grass-roots battles that created the momentum to win the hearts and support of the masses.

THE PEOPLE'S STRUGGLE

As was mentioned in chapter 5, one of the first movements that Gandhi became involved in upon his return to India was the protest against the exploitation of the peasants in the Champaran region. He was able to secure a rebate for the indigo workers of the outlandish sums of money accumulated by their British landlords.

He then went on to negotiate salary disputes on behalf of the textile workers in Ahmedabad. His campaign there was so successful that even the daughter of the mill owner took Gandhi's side and fought with him.

While the textile workers' negotiations were still in progress, Gandhi went to the Kheda district of Gujarat. The peasants there were starving because of poor crop yields. To add to their difficulties, it was time to pay the taxes on the very crops that were not even able to sustain them.

Gandhi's plea, mentioned in chapter 7, was for the commissioner to suspend the taxes for that particular year. During the struggle, the Government tried to coerce the peasants, confiscating their animals and goods. This only increased the peasants' determination and they held firm. In the end, Gandhi was able to persuade the Government to agree that the wealthier of the farmers would pay their taxes, and the poorer ones would have a reprieve. Unfortunately, it was up to the farmers to decide who would be the paying farmers and who would not. They refused to take on this responsibility, so it was only a half-hearted victory.

In these first two circumstances, Gandhi won what would become a typical victory for him – meaning that not all of his demands were met, but a reasonable compromise was concluded between the parties involved. The last however, did not meet with as much success.

Even so, Gandhi was stirring the people into action through these protests, and this gave them the inspiration and confidence to stand up to the powerful British Government. They were also beginning to understand the notion that it was their right to do so, which had not previously been the case for them. Before Gandhi, the masses, most of whom were incredibly poor and uneducated, only thought of themselves as victims of the sovereignty and incapable of challenging it.

GANDHI'S PUBLICATIONS

One of the ways that Mahatma Gandhi was able to reach the masses was through his publications. He had created a number of pamphlets that expressed his views on social reform and satyagraha. These began to have widespread readership.

The first of his publications was *Indian Opinion*, founded in 1903, which continued to be produced in South Africa by one of his sons. His document *Hind Swaraj* was the basis for his free India manifesto. It had been inspired and written in 1909 but it took a number of years to fully influence its readership.

The other two weekly pamphlets that were offered to him to use as an educational tool for the people were **Navajivan** and *Young India*. He became the editor of both. Later, in 1933, he put together a pamphlet specifically designed to address the discrimination of the Untouchables. It was called **Harijan**, which means 'God's children'.

KEYWORDS

Navajivan, an activist pamphlet edited by Gandhi.

Harijan, a pamphlet geared toward the Untouchables.

Gandhi understood that first he had to educate people about the situation. He also knew it was important to draw a lot of attention to his protests and campaigns. The thousands of people who supported him knew of his every move. This put a lot of pressure on the authorities, because the whole of India and much of the world was watching his progress. This is one of the reasons he was released from jail more than once, and at other times had his sentence reduced. The Government couldn't afford to mistreat the Mahatma with the entire country watching.

BECOMING THE LEADER OF THE CONGRESS IN 1920

Another factor in Mahatma Gandhi's success was his ability to bring different groups together. He was successful in establishing himself as the unrivalled leader of the Indian National Congress for many years. This was an important position for Gandhi because the Congress was at the time the largest Indian-organized and politically active group in the country. Although its members did not always agree with his tactics or ideas, they still let him take the lead. It was also here that he made numerous contacts with useful people. His networking in India began with his associations within the Congress, and it was this that contributed to making his campaigns prominent and successful.

THE BEGINNING OF MASS SATYAGRAHA

In 1921 Mahatma Gandhi presided over what was to be his first mass use satyagraha. He spent a year promoting non-cooperation with the British. The demonstrations included not buying British goods, not working in jobs controlled by the British, and not wearing any Western/British clothing. One of the major events he arranged was a huge bonfire in Bombay in the July of that year in which participants set light to British fabrics.

This was also the year that he led a boycott for the visit of the Prince of Wales. The political situation was very tense at this time. The Indian people were behind Gandhi's protests so much that the jails bulged with nearly thirty thousand demonstrators. He and his friend and colleague, Jawaharla Nehru, were among those arrested.

The difficulty with the mass satyagraha movement was that it sometimes precipitated violence throughout the country. So once again, the Mahatma cancelled the demonstrations. Stopping the protests if they became out of control was one of Gandhi's best negotiating tools. He needed the authorities to see that he did not condone violence and he also needed the people to see the same.

GANDHI–IRWIN PACT OF 1931

Gandhi's famous Salt March, described in the last chapter, incited most of the country to protest. Within three months of the march sixty to ninety thousand Indians were arrested for ignoring the salt laws. At least a hundred were killed and thousands wounded in the clashes that ensued because of people following Gandhi's example of harvesting salt from the beaches.

The Mahatma met with the viceroy, Lord Irwin, at least eight times in order to come to some kind of compromise over the situation. Initially, Gandhi had 11 issues that he wanted addressed and altered. He was not to get everything he wanted. However, he is quoted in *Gandhi and India* (see Further Reading) as saying that the satyagraha's intention is always to try to 'convert the adversary with love'. Compromises often had to be made, and it was this willingness to compromise that often angered Gandhi's supporters.

ASHRAMS

Gandhi's ashrams were both experiments in community living and headquarters for his political activism. His first and second ashrams (Phoenix and Tolstoy Farm) were built in South Africa. His third ashram was founded upon his return to India near Ahmedabad just slightly northeast of his birth place. He lived there until 1933. He says of his days there: 'Our creed was devotion to truth, and our business was the search for and insistence on truth. I wanted to acquaint India with the method I had tried in South Africa, and I desired to test in India the extent to which its application might be possible. So my companions and I selected the name 'Satyagraha Ashram' as conveying both our goal and our method of service.' In 1933 he moved from his Sabarmati residence to Wardha, in more central India. His new headquarters here he would call Sevagram, which meant 'village of service'.

It was during this time that the Mahatma decided to take more of a back seat in public politics. Instead, he focused his attentions on very practical internal problems, mainly the Untouchables situation and the Hindu–Muslim conflict. His idea was that in order to prepare India for independence, it needed to learn to be capable of handling its independence. This is where Gandhi's ideas of personal development and politics overlapped.

GIVING UP THE LEGAL PROFESSION

Throughout Gandhi's career he let his profession as a barrister take a back seat to his public work. Initially, he used his law practice to provide a living for himself and his family, and this gave him credence within society. His legal training helped teach him how to behave with the authorities. He became astute at dealing with leaders in high positions.

But practising law was never where his heart was. He was first and foremost interested in being with the common people and addressing their needs. He was absorbed in inspiring people to stand up for themselves and change their lives from within. He was committed to leading a life of few distractions and material possessions.

As the years passed, when he was imprisoned he listed his profession as 'weaver'. By the time he had given up practising law there was enough of a following behind him, that his day to day needs were handled by his devotees. It was not, though, handled without difficulty. Even though Gandhi's material wants were few, his protests and travels were costly. His good friend Sarojini Naidu once joked that he didn't have a clue how much it cost to keep him in poverty.

GOVERNMENT OF INDIA ACT

The last time the British Government would exclusively make rules for the Indian people was in 1935. A new constitution was initiated called the Government of India Act. It was

> **KEYWORD**
>
> **Suffrage**, the right to vote.

meant to give more autonomy to the local communities while the Raj still retained overall authority. The new reforms were to include **suffrage** for women and Untouchables. It also created a provincial congress of governments in 1937. The Act was also intended to create a federation between the different provinces, but this intention was never implemented.

The granting of suffrage to women and Untouchables gave the people a voice. The number of Indians voting rose from 6.5 million to 35 million. In the 1937–38 elections, the Congress won support by 70 per cent, thus making it into a bonafide political party. It was a party of the people. Its members included all social and economic sections of the population.

WAR

The breakout of the war in Europe in 1939 put a damper on the free India movement. It was a sensitive situation. The country was in turmoil. The Indians wanting their independence from their keepers would now be expected to sign up to help defend them in Europe. On the one hand, they didn't want to see Britain lose the war; on the other hand, Britain was the foe they were fighting. What made matters worse, was that the British Government did not consult the Indians before involving them.

In opposition to the war, Gandhi and many of his followers and members of the congress resigned from their positions of leadership and got themselves arrested. The leader of the Muslim league, Ali Jinnah, was of course, happy to see this because he felt he could bring his party to the forefront. He immediately set about procuring a resolution to separate India so that Muslims and Hindus could live independently of each other. The Muslim League were trying to take over as the voice of all India. This did not please the members of the Congress at all. Many were opposed to partitioning India, and no one more so than Gandhi.

THE CRIPPS INTERVENTION

The British Government sent Sir Stafford Cripps (1889–1952) to India with a proposal that was supposed to help ease tensions between the Congress and the Muslim League. The idea was that after the war, a self-governing Indian Union would be formed that each state could freely join. The problem with the plan was that it didn't do anything to alleviate the immediate problems between the two factions. In fact, it opened itself up to creating an even more separatist movement.

The Cripps intervention injected new energy into the anti-British campaigns. In 1942, the people relaunched its independence campaign with even more vigour than before. Demonstrations broke out in every corner of the country, introducing with them the new slogan 'Quit India!'

KASTURBAI'S DEATH

In the midst of all the progress that Gandhi and his followers were making, he lost his wife. Gandhi and his wife Kasturbai had been intellectual opposites. She had no education whatsoever, whereas he had learned a great deal. Kasturbai was a housewife which, as a Hindu woman, was her natural vocation. Because Gandhi saw her as his equal, he was intending to help educate her. Unfortunately, as with his sons, he never got around to doing so.

Even though Kasturbai was not able to discuss things with her husband as an equal, they were very dependent on each other. She was dependent upon him to take care of her and their family. He was dependent upon her to look after his needs. He required of her everything that he demanded of himself. This often created rows between them, but Kasturbai always succumbed to her husband's wishes in the end, and she was one of his staunchest supporters. When she died in 1944, he was devastated. He remarked: 'I cannot imagine life without Ba...Her passing has left a vacuum never to be filled...'.

INDIA'S EMANCIPATION AND PARTITION

The Congress was originally the stronger of the two nationalist parties until the start of the war. Then the Muslim League actively began to rally its members. By the end of the war it was now able to win 90 per cent of the votes in elections. Unfortunately, the Muslim League was very frustrated with the old constitutional methods of resolving conflict and instigated more direct actions, which usually included force. The situation between the two communities only got worse. Violence broke out in many cities and provinces and there was a lot of bloody rioting. Civil war had begun in India, resulting in many massacres. The country was in chaos.

The wheel is an ancient symbol meaning 'wheel of law' (left) India's national emblem, its inscription means 'truth alone triumphs' (right).

The situation in India had brought itself worldwide attention. Other countries were now expressing their opinions about India's independence. In February 1947, the British Government declared it would partition India and give it its freedom at midnight on 14 August, of that year.

It was a bitter-sweet victory for India. The horrible situation between the warring religious communities remained volatile. Hindus were leaving their homes to go and live in Hindu communities for fear for their lives. Muslims were doing the same. No one trusted each other. This was the greatest of blows for Gandhi. He never wanted to see his country divided in this way. He did not rejoice or celebrate on 14 August. Instead he undertook what would be his final fast as a campaign for tolerance between the religious communities. India had at long last gained its independence, but it was not a country at peace.

* * * *SUMMARY* * * *

- Mahatma Gandhi met with both successes and failures in all of the movements he started.

- The first pamphlet he created in South Africa was called *Indian Opinion.*

- His manifesto for Indian home rule was called *Hind Swaraj.*

- He was also the editor for the weekly publications, *Young India* and *Navajivan.*

- He created a publication specifically directed toward the Untouchables called *Harijan* which means 'God's children'.

- He was the unrivalled leader of the Congress for a number of years.

- He founded two ashrams in South Africa and two in India which were his social experiments with community living and his political headquarters.

- As his career progressed, he gave up his profession as a barrister.

- He was devastated by the loss of his wife Kasturbai in 1944.

- World War II slowed down the free India campaign.

- After the war, the fighting between the different religious groups in India intensified; massacres and riots occurred.

- In 1947, Britain partitioned India into two separate states.

- On 14 August at midnight, India gained her independence. This, however, did not solve the problems of civil war.

In His Own Words

I have nothing new to teach the world. Truth and non-violence are as old as the hills. All I have done is to try experiments in both on as vast a scale as I could.

M.K. Gandhi

Mahatma Gandhi was a very prolific writer. The *Collected Works of Mahatma Gandhi* alone spans 90 volumes. In this chapter we will take a look at some of his remarks on a wide range of topics. The quotations come from a variety of sources referenced in the Further Reading section. All quotations by Gandhi are the property of the Navajivan Trust, Ahmedabad, India.

ON EQUALITY WITH HIS WIFE

A Hindu upbringing taught Gandhi that women were the property of their husbands. He came to regret treating his wife in this way and developed an equal relationship with her. He also promoted the equality of all women. In speaking of his early years with his wife he said:

'But I was a cruelly kind husband. I regarded myself as her teacher and so harassed her out of my blind love for her.'

As their relationship grew so did their love and mutual respect.

'I am no longer a blind, infatuated husband. I am no more my wife's teacher. Kasturbai can, if she will, be as unpleasant to me [scold me] today as I used to be to her before. We are tried friends, the one no longer regarding the other as the object of lust...The incident in question occurred in 1898 when I had no conception ['no command'] of brahmacharya. It was a time when I thought that the wife was the object of her husband's lust, born to do her husband's behest, rather than a helpmate, a comrade and a partner in the husband's joys and sorrows.'

ON GOD AND TRUTH

Mahatma Gandhi was a spiritual seeker. He found his personal relationship with the Divine in his service to others.

'If God who is indefinable can be at all defined, then I should say that God is TRUTH. It is impossible to reach HIM, that is TRUTH, except through LOVE. LOVE can only be expressed fully when man reduces himself to a cipher. This process of reduction to cipher is the highest effort man or woman is capable of making. It is the only effort worth making, and it is possible only through ever-increasing self-restraint.'

'I want to see God face to face. God I know is Truth. For me the only means of knowing God is non-violence – ahimsa – love,…'

'I am here to serve no one else but myself, to find my own self-realisation through the service of these village folk. Man's ultimate aim is the realisation of God, and all His activities, social, political, religious, have to be guided by the ultimate aim of the vision of God. The immediate service of all human beings becomes a necessary part of the endeavour simply because the only way to find God is to see Him in His creation and be one with it. This can only be done by service of all...If I could persuade myself that I should find Him in a Himalayan cave, I would proceed there immediately. But I know that I cannot find Him apart from humanity.'

ON NON-VIOLENCE AND AHIMSA

Gandhi's guiding force was always to meet oppression with non-violent civil disobedience. He stood firmly by this and was willing to die himself rather than use force.

'Non-violence for me is not a mere experiment. It is part of my life and the whole creed of satyagraha, Non-co-operation, Civil Disobedience, and the like, are necessary deductions from the fundamental proposition that Non-violence is the law of life for human beings. For me it is both a means and an end and I am more than ever convinced that in the complex situation that faces India, there is no other way of gaining real freedom. In applying my mind to the present situation I must, therefore, test everything in terms of Non-violence.'

'Today perhaps I am the only one left who has faith in ahimsa. I pray to God that he may grant me the strength to demonstrate this ahimsa even if it be in my own person so it is all the same to me whether there are or there are not all these police and military personnel posted here for my protection. Because it is Rama who protects me...I become more and more convinced that everything else is futile.'

ON CIVIL DISOBEDIENCE

Mahatma Gandhi was influenced greatly by the works of Tolstoy, Thoreau, and Marx. These, along with his religious upbringing formed the basis of his experiments with civil disobedience and satyagraha.

'It is my firm belief that in the complex constitution under which we are living, the only safe and honourable course for a self-respecting man is, in the circumstances such as face me, to do what I have decided to do, that is, to submit without protest to the penalty of disobedience. I have ventured to make this statement not in any way of extenuation of the order served upon me, not for want of respect for lawful authority, but in obedience of the higher law of our being the voice of conscience.'

ON THE MEANS TO AN END

Consistency and constancy were two of Gandhi's greatest qualities. He never collapsed his principles under the weight of difficulties.

'Your belief that there is no connection between the means and the end is a great mistake. Through that mistake, even men who have been considered religious have committed grievous crimes. Our reasoning is the same as saying that we can get a rose through planting a noxious weed. If I want to cross the ocean, I can do so only by means of a vessel; if I were to use a cart for that purpose, both the cart and I would soon find the bottom...The means may be likened to a seed, the end to a tree; and there is just the same inviolable connection between the means and the end as there is between the seed and the tree.'

ON RELIGIOUS TOLERANCE

Throughout his career Gandhi's greatest wish was for the cooperation and tolerance of the religions in India. He felt this was even more important than the move to free India from British rule.

'I regard both the religions as equally true with my own. But my own gives me full satisfaction. It contains all that I need for my growth. It teaches me to pray not that others may believe as I believe but that they may grow to their full height in their own religion. My constant prayer therefore is for a Christian or a Muslim to be a better Christian and a better Mohammedan. I am convinced, I know, that God will ask, asks us now, not what we label ourselves, but what we are, i.e., what we do.

'...all religions are more or less God-given...therefore one must work out one's own salvation in the religion of one's own forefathers; for, a seeker after Truth finds out that all religions melt and become one in god who is one and the same for all His creatures.'

ON DHARMA (DUTY OF RELIGION) AND THE MORALITY OF ACTIONS

Self-restraint, tolerance and good deeds were primary aspects of Gandhi's life and work. He never wavered from these ideals and he practised what he preached.

'Unfortunately a belief has today sprung up that one's private character has nothing to do with one's public activity. This superstition must go. Our public workers must set about the task of reforming society by reforming themselves first. This spiritual weapon of self-purification, intangible as it seems, is the most potent means for revolutionizing one's environment and for loosening external shackles.'

'The way... is to do pure and good deeds; to have compassion for all living things, and to live in truth. Even after reaching this stage, one does not attain liberation, for one has to enjoy embodied existence as a consequence of one's good deeds as well. One has, therefore, to go a step further. We will, however, have to continue to act, only we should not cherish any attachment to our actions. Action should be undertaken for its own sake, without an eye on the fruit. In short, everything should be dedicated to God.'

ON THE BRITISH IN INDIA

Gandhi grew up proud to be considered a citizen of the British Empire. Later he met with some ambiguities in how he would be able to remain respectful of British rule while trying to change it and to free India of its reign.

'[You] want English rule without the Englishman. You want the tiger's nature, not the tiger; that is to say, you would make India English. And when it becomes English, it will be called not Hindustan but Englistan. This is not the Swaraj [Self rule, home rule] I want.'

'The foreign power will be withdrawn before long, but for me real freedom will come only when we free ourselves of the dominance of Western education, Western culture and [the] Western way of living which have been ingrained in us, because this culture has made our living expensive and artificial...Emancipation from this culture would mean real freedom for us.'

ON INDIA'S INDEPENDENCE

The following is part of what Gandhi said to the West Bengal ministers on 15 August 1947, the first day of Indian Independence.

'From today you have to wear the crown of thorns. Strive ceaselessly to cultivate truth and non-violence. Be humble. Be forbearing. The British rule no doubt put you on your mettle. But now you will be tested through and through. Beware of power; power corrupts. Do not let yourselves be entrapped by its pomp and pageantry. Remember, you are in office to serve the poor in India's villages. May God help you.'

ABOUT HIMSELF

Gandhi's 'experiments with truth' trace his growth as a personality, a religious man and as a leader.

'My bent is not political but religious and I take part in politics because I feel that there is no department of life which can be divorced from religion and because politics touch the vital being of India almost at every point.'

'I claim to be a simple individual liable to err like any other fellow mortal. I own, however, that I have humility enough in me to confess my errors and to retrace my steps. I own that I have immovable faith in God and His goodness and unconsumable passion for truth and love. But, is that not what every person has latent in him?'

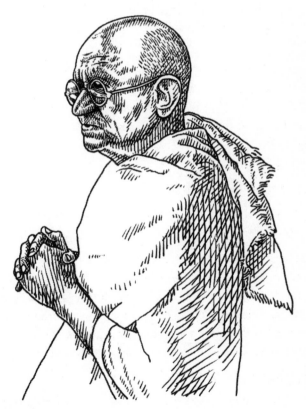

Gandhi as an older man.

✻ ✻ ✻ ✻ SUMMARY ✻ ✻ ✻ ✻

- Gandhi regretted initially treating his wife as property and said that 'her matchless powers of endurance have always been the victor'.

- He said that 'man's ultimate aim is the realization of God'.

- He felt that 'non-violence is the law of life for human beings'.

- Gandhi believed that the 'voice of conscience' was the 'honourable course for a self-respecting man'.

- He taught that there is an 'inviolable connection between the means and the end' and that was why non-violence was of paramount importance.

- He thought that real freedom for India would come from embracing its own culture and not Western culture.

- Gandhi warned India's new leaders to beware of power because 'power corrupts'.

His Assassination and Legacy

Truth quenches untruth, love quenches anger, self-suffering quenches violence. This eternal rule is a rule not for saints but for all.

M.K. Gandhi

Being a legend in one's own time is not without its hardships, both personal and private. Gandhi, however, seemed to thrive on a life of self-sacrifice and renunciation. For the most part he didn't mind that he had little private life, though he did regret losing time he could have spent with his family. The happiness of his family was very important to him. He, himself, was happiest when he was living life as simply as possible, helping the poor, and inspiring people to protest against their oppressive conditions.

As a youth, his family had encouraged him to gain a degree in law so he could take a prestigious job within his community as his father had done. Little did they know that this training would ignite a flame in him that would lead him to become an international figure. He wasn't looking for prestige, he was looking for justice. Gandhi soon realized that law was simply a means to an end. That means was knowing enough about the law that he could mount successful protests against human rights violations. Being an educated man also gave him some credence in Western society. His education and contacts opened many doors for him.

HIS FOUR SONS

He was devoted to his family even though he was often separated from them for periods of time. As was mentioned earlier, he was a very maternal man and gladly took part in the care of his children. He was not so much concerned that they get a formal education as an education in 'life'. He meant to take on giving them a formal education himself, but admitted that he never had enough time to devote to it.

He would later recognize that this put them at a disadvantage in the world, of which they were very aware.

His eldest son Harilal left the family at an early age. He converted to Islam to defy his father. He also married against his father's wishes and sadly his wife met with an early death. That, combined with the death of his young son, drove him to alcoholism. He was never to make anything of his life and died of tuberculosis four months after Gandhi's assassination.

After Gandhi had settled in India, he sent his second son Manilal back to South Africa to continue his work on *Indian Opinion*, the paper that he had begun there. Manilal lived out most of his life in Africa, lonely to be away from his family. When the Mahatma was assassinated, he was too far away to make it back for the funeral.

Gandhi's other two younger sons, Ramdas and Devadas, worked for their father in India. They effectively supported his causes and worked for them until he died. None of his four sons ever wrote anything about their relationship with their father. One explanation that was given by his wife was that the Mahatma was too busy being everyone's father to spend enough time with his own children. Interestingly, she didn't criticize him for this, she felt his job was to look after the whole world.

HIS ADOPTED DAUGHTERS
Gandhi's extended family reached out to include his two grandnieces, Manu and Abha. They were orphans whom he raised. He was especially fond of Manu. In his older years he was constantly in their company. They were his caretakers and companions. He relied particularly heavily on them after Kasturbai died. They were both with him in his last few moments of life. They loved him dearly and called him by the endearment, Bapu.

FRIENDS AND COLLEAGUES
Mahatma Gandhi met with many people throughout his career. Most were the very poorest of India and some were national and international leaders:

* Jawaharlal Nehru (1889–1964) was a friend and colleague of Gandhi's who would go on to become the Prime Minister of India when it gained its independence.

* Indira Gandhi (1917–84) was Jawaharlal Nehru's daughter. She was not related to Mahatma Gandhi. Her name came through marriage to a man named Feroze Shah Gandhi who died in 1960 and left her with two sons, Rajiv and Sanjay. She went on to become the Prime Minister of India.

* Annie Besant (1847–1933) was one of the founders of the Theosophical Society. She became very involved in the movement for India's independence.

* Rabindranath Tagore (1861–1941) was a distinguished Bengali poet who ran a school and won the Nobel Prize in 1913. He and Gandhi met and corresponded regularly over the years even though their ideology did not necessarily converge.

* Ali Jinnah (1876–1948) was a very wealthy lawyer who lived in near Bombay in a palatial house. He became one of the most prominent leaders of the Muslim League even though he was not an orthodox Muslim. He was fully committed to and obsessed with the partitioning of India.

* Bal Gagandhar Talik (1856–1920) was an Indian nationalist leader. He was an orthodox Hindu who was committed to using violence.

* Sarojini Naidu (1879–1949) was an Indian poet and political activist. She was known by the beautiful silk saris she wore. She was very involved with the Indian independence movement and travelled to London as part of Gandhi's entourage for the Round Table Conference.

* Romain Rolland (1866–1944) was a European author who wrote a book about Gandhi in his early career. His interest in Gandhi brought him much renown throughout Europe.

A SCANDAL

When Mahatma Gandhi was in his seventies a scandal occurred. He was discovered naked in bed with his grandniece who was also naked. She was not the only one of his followers to have been found in such a manner. Apparently a number of his women followers had kept him company through the night. There are a few different versions of this episode.

Gandhi apparently explained it away in a very vague manner. With one breath he said that he was old and needed the warmth. His other explanation was that it was a test of his celibacy. He denied ever having sex with any of the women.

No one will ever know (excepting the women who had shared his bed) what exactly went on, but the scandal lost him the respect of some of his devotees.

GANDHI'S PREMONITION ABOUT DEATH

On the last day of his life, at the age of 78, Mahatma Gandhi woke early as usual to follow his very disciplined daily routine. His days were filled with prayer and meditation, meetings with leaders and visitors.

Interestingly he made three references to not living much longer throughout this day according to the International Gandhi Movement. The first instance was in the later morning when his grandniece Manu offered him some allopathic lozenges for his bad cough because they had run out of his herbal ones. He of course refused because he shunned conventional medicine. He replied to her: 'Who knows what is going to happen before nightfall or even whether I shall be alive. If at night I am still alive you can easily prepare some then.'

The second incident occurred when he was talking to a delegation of Muslim leaders with whom he had been meeting daily. He was talking with them about some travel plans for a conference in Delhi he was due to attend. He said to them: 'I do expect to be back here by the 14th. But if Providence has decreed otherwise, that is a different matter. I am not, however sure whether I shall be able to leave here even on the day after tomorrow. It is all in God's hands.'

The Mahatma's third comment about his potential demise was when Manu inquired whether or not he could see some other visitors that day. Gandhi replied to Manu's request saying: 'Tell them that I will, but only after the prayer meeting, and that too if I am still living.'

To some it may seem a bit more than a coincidence that he should speak about his death on the very day that he was to die. Perhaps it was because there had been other failed attempts to take his life throughout his career. In fact, just ten days prior, there had been an attempt during an evening prayer meeting at Gandhi's home, Birla House. Or perhaps he was having premonition that his life was ending.

NATHURAM GODSE

Nathuram Godse's name was to become known throughout India on 30 January 1948. He was a 37-year-old Hindu extremist who had been part of the 20 January conspiracy to assassinate Gandhi. He, along with two conspirators, Narayan Apte and Vishnu Karkare, were preparing to make good their scheme this time. There were actually eight men involved altogether, but it was these three who were to carry it out.

Godse travelled separately from Apte and Karkare to Birla House. Their original plan was for Godse to shoot Gandhi while he was on a platform holding a prayer meeting. The other two were to be planted in the crowd to intercede in case any one tried to interfere. Since the other assassination attempt Gandhi had agreed to have some 30 policemen stationed at Birla House, but he would not go so far as to give them the power to search people. It was therefore easy for Godse to get in to the meeting carrying a revolver.

The Mahatma was deep in a conversation with Sadar Patel (Minister of Internal Affairs under Nehru), but ended it in order to go to his prayer meeting. He was being guided by his two grandnieces Manu and Abha. Usually there were three or so other people who walked in front of

Gandhi or by his side as he walked, but today only Manu and Abha were there.

Because he was late he walked a different route to the platform where the crowd of several hundred were waiting for him. As he was walking along the path Godse noticed he was coming right towards him. Instead of keeping to the original plan, he decided to take his moment. He stepped out and approached the Mahatma with his palms pressed together. This was the usual form of greeting. He bowed to Gandhi and greeted him. His grandniece thought Godse was going to kiss Gandhi's feet, which was something Gandhi did not like, so she began to motion him away. She was irritated with him and began to argue with him. At that moment she dropped the rosary she was carrying so she bent to pick it up. Godse took his chance. He fired three times at close range. All three bullets hit Gandhi in the abdomen and chest. As he began to fall to the ground it is reported that the Mahatma uttered 'He Ram, He Ram' which means 'oh God, oh God'. He lay with his head on the two girls' laps for only a few moments and then he died.

On the evening of Gandhi's death, his good friend, colleague and the Prime Minister of India, Nehru, spoke to India on the radio. In his address he said:

> The light has gone out of our lives and there is darkness everywhere and I do not quite know what to tell you and how to say it. Our beloved leader, Bapu, as we call him, the Father of our Nation is no more. Perhaps I am wrong to say that. Nevertheless, we will not see him again as we have seen him these many years. We will not run to him for advice and seek solace from him, and that is a terrible blow not to me only but to millions and millions in this country. And it is difficult to soften the blow by any advice that I or anyone else can give you.

> The light has gone out, I said, and yet I was wrong, for the light that shone in this country was no ordinary light...and a thousand years later

that light will still be seen in this country, and the world will see it...For that light represented the living truth...

from Louis Fischer, *Life of Mahatma Gandhi*, 1951

THE MAHATMA'S FUNERAL

Thousands of people turned out to see the Mahatma lying in state on top of Birla House before his cremation. Two hundred soldiers escorted his body to the site where he was to be cremated. At the **pyre** site there were two million Indians watching as his body was burnt.

> **KEYWORDS**
>
> **Prototype,** a person or thing that serves as an example of a type.
>
> **Pyre,** a pile of wood or combustible material for cremating a corpse.

The next day his ashes were collected by his family. Ten days later they took them to India's holiest of rivers, the Ganges, where surrounded by a large crowd they released his ashes.

GANDHI'S LEGACY

Mahatma Gandhi accomplished a great deal in his 78 years. He greatly influenced the Indian and black culture in South Africa. He gave them the courage and the confidence to stand up for themselves. He was the first to make a tangible difference to their situation. He fought for their human rights and he returned them their dignity. His acts of civil disobedience towards prejudicial laws produced a **prototype** that he would be able to use in his mother country as well.

In India, he was fundamental in publicly objecting to the caste discrimination of the Untouchables. Their acceptance in society was one of his primary quests. He saw all beings as equals. He was blind to discrimination on any grounds.

His fasts were a completely new concept as a form of political protest. He always undertook his fasts with complete seriousness and dedication. They were not merely attention-seeking devices. Each time he fasted he was prepared to die for what he believed.

0   200 km   London to Bombay 4,473 miles

On the question of home rule for India, it was Gandhi who led the first campaign. The concept at the time was like David meeting Goliath – one man taking on an Empire – but he proved that the underdog could win.

The Mahatma was always against the partition of India. His dream was that all religious factions would be able to live together peacefully. He was not to see his dream fulfilled. He was very disappointed when India gained her independence, but became a divided country with Hindus and Muslims living separately. This conflict did not right itself in Gandi's time, nor has it today.

Much of what Gandhi had lived to see change, remains immutable. This doesn't mean that his life was in vain. He did make a sizable impact, and although some of his ideas may seem idealistic or simplistic, his experiments with truth did yield results.

The legacy that he left behind is also in his writings. His complete works, which fill over 90 volumes, continue to be published today in both Hindi and English.

✳ ✳ ✳ ✳ SUMMARY ✳ ✳ ✳ ✳

- Mahatma Gandhi was happy leading a life of self-sacrifice and denial.

- He liked being in jail because it gave him time to read and reflect.

- He had four sons; Harilal, Manilal, Ramdas and Devadas but he never had enough time to spend with them.

- He created a scandal when he was found naked in bed with his grandniece Manu when he was in his seventies.

- On the day of his assassination he spoke three different times about perhaps not being alive much longer.

- He was assassinated by a Hindu extremist named Nathuram Godse on 30 January 1948 on his way to a prayer meeting.

- Thousands came to Birla House to see him lie in state before his funeral.

- Two million Indians watched as his funeral pyre was lit.

- Ten days later, his relatives took his ashes and poured them in the holy river, the Ganges.

- The main causes he fought for were: the Untouchables, home rule for India, civil disobedience, religious tolerance and the search for truth.

Further Reading

The books listed here are a limited selection of those which should prove useful as a follow-up to issues touched on in this book.

GANDHI'S WRITINGS

All Men are Brothers, Columbia University Press, New York, 1959

The Collected Works of Mahatma Gandhi, 90 vols. Publications Division, Government of India, New Delhi, 1958–1984

An Autobiography, Or, My Experiments with Truth, Beacon Press, Boston, 1993

Gandhi in India in His Own Words, M. Green (ed.), University Press of New England, New Hampshire, 1987

Gandhi on Non-violence, T. Merton (ed.), New Directions, New York, 1965

Hind Swaraj and Other Writings, A. Parel (ed.), Cambridge University Press, Cambridge, 1997

Mahatma Gandhi and Leo Tolstoy Letters, B.S. Murthy (ed.) Long Beach Publications, Long Beach, California, 1987

The Moral and Political Writings of Mahatma Gandhi, 3 vols, D. Dalton (ed.), Clarendon Press, Oxford, 1986–1987

Selected Political Writings, D. Dalton (ed.), Hackett, Indianapolis, Indiana, 1996

BOOKS

An Introduction to Hinduism, Gavin Flood, Cambridge University Press, Cambridge, 1996

The Elements of World Religions, Liz Flower, Element Books, Dorset, 1997

From Samarkand to Stornoway Living Islam, Akbar S. Ahmed, BBC Books, London, 1993

Gandhi, Father of a Nation, Catherine, Clement, Thames and Hudson, 1996 (Oakwood)

Gandhi and India, Gianni, Sofri, Windrush Press, Gloucestershire, 1999 (Morley)

Gandhi, Prisoner of Hope, Judith, Brown, Yale University Press, New Haven and London, 1989 (Crossgates)

Gandhi's Significance for Today, The Elusive Legacy, edited, John Hick, and Lamont C. Hempel, Macmillan Press Ltd, London, 1989 (Guisely)

Gandhi's Truth, on the origins of militant nonviolence, Erik H. Erikson, Faber and Faber, London, 1970 (Central)

Hinduism, R.C. Zaehner, Oxford University Press, Oxford, 1966

India, A Concise History, Francis Watson, Thames and Hudson, 1979

The Life of Mahatma Gandhi, Louis Fischer, HarperCollins, 1997

Raj, The Making and Unmaking of British India, James, Lawrence, Little Brown & Co, London, 1997

ELECTRONIC RESOURCES

'The History of India' Web Page
www.indiagov.org/culture/history/intro.htm

'The Last Hours of Mahatma Gandhi' by Stephen Murphy
www.mkgandhi-sarvodaya.org

M.K. Gandhi
www.tick.information.uni-stuttgart.de/gangultr/india/mahatma.html

Mahatma Gandhi Album – Kamat's Potpourri Home Page
Assorted Quotes of Mahatma Gandhi
www.kamat.com/mmgandhi/mkgquote.htm

The Mind of Mahatma Gandhi – Neither Saint nor Sinner
www.ourindia.com/gandhi.htm

Glossary

Activism   Policy of taking direct action to achieve an end.

Ascetic   A person who practises self-denial (especially for religious purposes).

Atheism   Rejection of belief in God or gods.

Autobiography   Account of a person's life written by that person.

Ayurveda   Ancient Indian art of medicine.

Besant (Annie) [1847–1933]   One of the founders of the Theosophical movement and India Home Rule League.

Blavatsky (Madame)   One of the founders of the Theosophical Society.

Boycott   To refuse to have dealings with a thing or person.

British Empire   The United Kingdom and the territories under its control.

Buddhism   Asian religion founded by Gautama Buddha whereby man seeks enlightenment by denying greed, hatred and other causes of suffering.

Celibate   A person who abstains from sex.

Defame   Attack the good name or reputation of someone or something.

Democracy   A country governed by its people or their elected representatives.

Dharma   Custom regarded as a religion or moral duty.

Dhoti   Men's wrap-around trousers.

Dominion   Name formerly given to a self-ruling division of the British Empire.

Dyspepsia   Indigestion or stomach upset.

Elite   The most powerful or gifted members of a group or community.

Extremism   Supporting fanatical or radical political opinions.

Fakir   Religious beggar or ascetic.

Guru A religious teacher or leader giving personal spiritual guidance.

Hindu Belonging to the religion of Hinduism, the dominant religion of India.

Holistic Body, mind and spirit.

Homeopathy the treatment of disease by minute doses of drugs that in a healthy person would produce symptoms of the disease.

Hydrotherapy Method of treating illness using water.

Indenture A deed or sealed agreement between two or more parties.

Irrigate To supply land with water by means of artificial canals to promote the growth of crops.

Jain A person whose religion is Jainism, an ancient religion founded in India.

Jaundice Yellowing of the skin due to abnormal presence of bile pigments in the blood.

Jew A person whose religion is Judaism; member of the Semitic people descended from the ancient Israelites.

Karma Principle of retributive justice for past deeds.

Manifesto Public declaration of intent, policy, aims etc.

Monopoly Exclusive control of the supply of a product or service.

Muslim Follower of the religion of Islam, second-most important religion in India.

Marx (Karl) [1818–83] Thinker and writer who developed the concept of socialism.

Nomadic Wandering from place to place (to find pasture and food).

Orange Free State State in South Africa in the north of the country.

Parsee A person whose religion is Zoroastrianism, which was founded by an ancient Persian prophet named Zoroaster.

Pneumonia Inflammation of one or both lungs in which the air sacs become filled with liquid.

Poultice A paste of herbs held on the body with a cloth.

Prototype A person or thing that serves as an example of a type.

Pyre   A pile of wood or combustible material for cremating a corpse.

Quarantine   Period of isolation or detention.

Sage   Someone revered for his/her profound wisdom.

Sikh   Member of Indian religion that separated from Hinduism in the fifteenth century.

Semitic   Of Arabic and Judaic origins.

Socialism   Economic theory or system in which the means of production, distribution and exchange are owned by the community collectively.

Subcontinent   A large land mass that is a distinct part of a continent.

Suffrage   The right to vote.

Swardeshi   Using only indigenous good and materials.

Theosophical Society   Modern religious movement based on intuition and spiritual ecstasy.

Thoreau (Henry David) [1817–62] American author who wrote about civil disobedience.

Tolstoy (Leo) [1829–1910] Russian author and playwright.

Turban   A man's headdress worn especially by Hindus, Muslims and Sikhs.

Typhoid   Acute infectious disease characterized by fever, skin rash and headache.

Untouchables   Lowest of Hindu social classes.

Viceroy   Governor of a colony or province who rules in the name of the government.

Yoga   Hindu system of philosophy aimed at uniting the self with the Supreme Being through physical and mental exercises.

INDEX